ODE TO

Outhouse

WORDS OF WISDOM
FROM MY DRILL SERGEANT
AND MY UNCLE CLYDE

TOM EDWARDS

UNCLE CLYDE
PUBLISHING
Coshocton, Ohio

Many of these stories previously appeared,
in edited form, in the *Coshocton Tribune*,
Coshocton, Ohio.

Ode to the Outhouse
ISBN 978-0-615-39166-3

Coshocton, Ohio

DEDICATION

Once when I was a young Army Captain, pulling duty along the Communist Iron Curtain on the Czechoslovakian border, I looked through my binoculars and saw a Russian Captain looking through his binoculars looking back at me. I thought to myself, what is this Russian thinking? Twenty-Five years later through a Rotary International Exchange program a group of Russians visited Coshocton for a week. Two of the Russians had been in the Communist Red Army stationed in Czechoslovakia during the time frame I was there. I told them through the U.S. State Department interpreter about my Iron Curtain binocular incident.

All the Russians started laughing. They said when they looked across the border at the American soldiers; they saw our tactical nuclear missiles, tanks and artillery aimed at them. The Russian were trained to hate Americans, we were the enemy, the bourgeoisie; but they were not preoccupied by the geopolitical landscape. The Russians were impressed by our e sprit de corps. They said we seemed happy and smiled a lot. They wanted to come over the border and join us for a beer, listen to Radio Free Europe, get to know us and find out more about America. They had heard about American freedom and opportunities. The Russians just reinforced what I have known all along; how lucky I am to be an American.

I might poke fun at our Army Generals, our schools, and gripe about taxes, insurance, and lots of other things. I especially like to criticize our politicians even though "I are one" (I am honored to serve on the Coshocton City Council). But only in America could a dirt poor country boy work his way up to the best job in the world, owning a Hardware Store with great employees and loyal customers. As corny as this may sound: I dedicate this book to the United States of America.

C-130 rollin' down the strip,

Airborne daddy gonna take a little trip.

Stand up, buckle up, shuffle to the door,

jump right out and count to four.

If my chute don't open wide,

I'll be splattered on the countryside.

CONTENTS

continued on next page…

PREFACE

One of the most inspirational times in my youth was when I would be on the family farm, sitting in our two hole outhouse, thumbing through the Sears and Roebuck Catalog and dreaming of some day being able to work and eventually own my own hardware store.

Thanks to God, my Grandmothers, my Army Boot Camp Drill Sergeant and an understanding wife, my dreams came true.

I had jotted down little notes to myself along the way that were funny that I though that someday I could share with others.

I enrolled in a class about writing short stories at the Coshocton Pomerene Center for the Arts to polish my writing skills and to keep me out of the VFW at nights. If you enjoy my writings, please make a donation to the:

> Pomerene Center for the Arts
> 317 Mulberry
> Coshocton, OH 43812

Tom Edwards
auerace@clover.net

INTRODUCTION

Much of my youth was spent on the Edwards family farm in south Central Kentucky, near Abraham Lincoln's Birthplace. I loved living and working on the farm, hunting and shooting and going to Bales' Hardware Store every Saturday morning with my grandfather.

In High School I decided I wanted to go into the Army, shoot big guns and see the world. After my military service I would buy the family farm and then after a few good years of farming, buy or start my own hardware store.

No one in my family had ever been to college, but I had an uncle who was a sergeant in the Army. He talked me into applying for an Army R.O.T.C. college scholarship at Western Kentucky University. I was awarded the Army Scholarship and with the help of two part time jobs, I paid for my degree in Industrial Education.

As it turned out, it was good that I went to college, because the U.S. Surgeon General had released warnings in the late 1960's about smoking and tobacco products. Since our only cash crop on the farm was Tobacco, I could see the farm was not going to provide me with a future.

One of the Cadets in my R.O.T.C. rifle platoon was Romeo Crennel. Romeo has three Super Bowl Rings that he earned as the assistant coach of the New England Patriots and is now the head coach of the Cleveland

Browns.

In the summer of 1969 I did my Boot Camp at Indian Town Gap Military Reservation in Pennsylvania. Ten years later, my tour of duty at Indian Town Gap would help me get a date with my wife Karen.

I graduated from college in the fall of 1970 and reported for active duty three days later at the Army Infantry Officers School in Fort Benning, Ga. as a wet behind the ears, "Butter Bar" (2nd Lieutenant). One of the smartest things I did was sign up to have a $100.00 U.S. Savings Bond taken out of my pay and sent to my mother each month. That money would help finance my career later. After Officer School I went on to Paratrooper School and earned my Airborne Wings. I had orders to a replacement attachment in Long Bin, Viet Nam, but first had to pull 120 days of troop duty with the 4th Infantry Division at Fort Carson Colorado. The war in Viet Nam was changing and my orders were delayed for two years.

At Fort Carson I trained a Mechanized Platoon for war in the Middle East. We were secretly mustered one day for shipment to Israel. We were packed and sat on the tarmac of Peterson Air Force Base for a week, but never deployed. There was never a word about this in the media.

Growing up in the segregated South, I had some prejudice. The Army did a good job of teaching race relations and was very much color blind when it came to promotions and accommodations. I was honored to be selected by my Brigade to interview for the Jr. Aide de Camp for our new Assistant Division Commander, Gen.

Hamilton who happened to be black.

You make friends from all over America in the Army. My friend Lieutenant Bernie Zeper was from New York, Jewish and a West Point graduate who married a Las Vegas showgirl named Candy, who was brought up in the Mormon faith. Sergeant Brown was Black. He had dropped out of High School and been involved in an armed robbery in South Chicago. The judge gave Brownie a choice of jail or enlist in the Army. Brownie found a home in the Army with the discipline, honor and duty; he earned his GED and was taking college courses at night. Bernie and Brownie were good beer drinking buddies and we played on the same Battalion volley ball team. I wish judges today used their bench to force young men who are in trouble, looking for a home and a purpose into the military.

In 1973 I received orders for Viet Nam again. Thirty days from departure, my orders were changed and I was sent to Stuttgart, Germany. In Germany I was promoted to Captain and assigned to an experimental unit with the mission to convert the Army's tactical logistics to a computer, depot direct delivery system. I was picked to be a liaison between the computer programmer/systems analysts and the ordinary soldier and tank mechanics. I wrote field manuals explaining how to input key punch cards into a rudimentary IBM field computer that took two semi-trucks to haul.

Our Commanding Officers made us tour castles, attend operas, symphonies, museums and travel around Europe. I traveled to the border with Czechoslovakia many times. I would look through my binoculars at the Russian soldiers across the "Iron Curtain". I would wonder what my enemy was really like, what made him tick. In 1999 after the Iron curtain fell, the Coshocton Rotary Club hosted five Russians for a week of vocational training. One of the Russians had served in the Red army and had been in a tank unit on the Czech border. We laughed at how stupid the Iron Curtain had been and celebrated peace between our two countries with several shots of what he called cheap vodka, at the Coshocton Town and Country Club bar.

The most beautiful, yet disturbing country I traveled to was Yugoslavia (now Bosnia). There were Muslins, Christians and a large troop of Gypsies around Dubrovnik. They lived in different parts of the city and they all hated each other. Only the strong hands of Marshall Tito keep order then. I am proud our country, with the help of N.A.T.O., stopped the bloodshed in the Balkans. I am proud of our soldiers today who are trying to give peace a chance in Iraq and Afghanistan.

In our free country we can second guess our President and the Secretary of Defense and I do at times. Today we have retired Generals bad mouthing the Secretary of Defense. We have never had a military coup in America, because the military is run by civilians. Generals should "be seen and not heard". Abraham Lincoln said it best when he said "America is the Last Best Hope for Earth". I think it is our duty to promote freedom when we can, using force if necessary.

After my discharge from the Army, I started a career as a traveling Hardware Salesman. My territory was East Central Ohio. A couple who owned a store in Belmont County took a liking to me. One reason was Pete Rosnick had pulled his Word War II boot camp at Indian Town Gap, just as I had. Our commonality led him to fix me up on a blind date with his niece, Karen.

Karen and I were later married and had Erika. I wanted to fulfill my dreams of having my own store. We learned that Auer ACE Hardware was for sale in Coshocton. We visited, loved Coshocton, and bought the store (with the help of the Savings Bonds I sent my mother while in the Army and the money Karen had earned working several jobs). I have been very fortunate for the last 25 years. Coshocton has been good to my family.

I owe the Army a lot. I think there are a lot of young people in Coshocton that could benefit from military service. After all, in how many countries can a poor farm boy go to college, be a captain in the Army and own his childhood dream business? How many countries? Not many.

ODE TO THE OUTHOUSE

———▣———

As I was riding my bicycle, in the Stewart Addition, I saw an outhouse behind a modern house with an immaculate lawn. I had a flashback to my youth and our farm's two holer. After a closer look, this was merely a replica of an outhouse and in fact was a potting shed. With a small wind mill standing by the side, this back yard was transformed into a typical back yard of fifty years ago.

After we had indoor plumbing installed in the farm house, we kept the outhouse as a back up for several years. With 7 people in the family, the white porcelain indoor toilet was often occupied, mainly by my sister. Rather than fight with Sis, we just used the path. Our indoor bathroom, previously a closet, was small. Some large boned relatives, like Uncle Clyde, had difficulty maneuvering in such a small room. Uncle Clyde had to unsnap his bib suspender and drop his pants in the hallway before entering the bathroom. He claimed there wasn't enough room to assume the position with the bathroom door shut.

In the Army I had to share 10 toilets with 40 other guys. There were no partitions between them, so we learned to be uninhibited during our "daily." When on bivouac we used our trenching tool (shovel) to dig our own latrines in the earth and use little bitty squares of tissue that were packed with our c-rations.

1

Once out of the Army, I got married, had a kid and bought a big house with big bathrooms. I became spoiled with this city living, until I had to replace an older toilet with one of the new 1.5 gallon water saver toilets.

With an outhouse, gravity took care took flushing. Then with a Sears and Roebuck Catalog page or a corn cob, you pull up your pants, out the door and onto your work. With the 3.5 gallon toilets, you pushed down the flush handle and you were done.

With the new 1.5 gallon toilets, flushing is more of an adventure. Congress mandated these damn toilets. Their reasoning was that it cost lots of money to build more sewer treatment plants, so if they cut the amount of water used to flush, no need for new sewer plants. The money saved could be used to increase congressmen's pay, build new government buildings in D.C. and dig a subway under our nation's capitol that no one would use.

I don't know who tested the new water saver toilets. Maybe they tested them where no one eats solid food, a liquid diet resort or somewhere? A normal person can not use these low volume toilets without lots of flush attempts and the use of a plunger.

To make matters worse, we now see automatic flush levers on public toilets. Apparently we are not to be trusted with the task of flushing manually. We have an electronic eye tell the toilet when we are done.

I am sure some of these computer chips electronic eyes work, but I always get the ones that malfunction. They flush uncontrollably and cause me to have to kick the black box into submission after I call it a few names.

I sometimes get the reluctant models. I wave my hands, stand up, sit down, and call it names until finally it wakes up and flushes.

I am scared to go to friends' houses anymore. I am afraid if nature calls, I may embarrass myself. Nothing is more embarrassing than to exit the bathroom at a party and have to find the home owner to ask where their plunger is located.

When my daughter was growing up, I always asked her to use our bathroom before we left the house. Now I find I am asking myself, do I have to go, before I leave the house. I guess progress, or water savers, make me a better planner if nothing else.

Raisin' Kids

—◻—

With the mobile life that we now live, extended families are becoming a thing of the past. I wasn't that long ago those Grandparents played a vital role in raising their grandchildren. Grandparents now head to places like Padre Island, Texas or Vero Beach, Florida for the winter. Aunts and Uncles who often times lived on the next farm or over the ridge or at least in the same county played a role in rearing youngins too. They now live in places like Atlanta or Minneapolis. They moved to cities where there were jobs and opportunities.

Sure families get together for reunions once in a while. Families make Christmas season the most traveled time of the year via interstate highways and airports, but it's not the same. Occasional get togethers are too polite. There is not enough time for cousins to size each other up and get in to mischief (a true bonding experience). No time to figure out which uncles you don't like and which ones you can work to get things from that your parents won't let you have. No time to figure out which Aunt likes to hug and kiss, thereby embarrassing you in front of the whole clan.

Growing up in Pascal on our family farm, all family members helped raise me. Grandfather taught me how to use hand tools from an axe, sledge, and wedge, to a synath, corn knife, and spade. Grandfather taught me that nothing is accomplished without callous, elbow grease, and using your noggin (head). My father taught me how to use a rifle, shotgun, and fishing pole. Nothing makes you feel more important when you are twelve years old, than to sit down at a family dinner where the fish, fowl, or game on the table were a product of your efforts, which included skinning or filleting.

Grandmother taught me how to darn my own socks and crochet. She taught me how to pick beans, snap beans, cold pack beans and store beans in the cellar. She taught me how to butcher a hog and smoke hams. She taught me how to wash in a wash tub including behind my ears. Most of all she taught me to fear the lord.

Uncle Clyde was in charge of sanding the rough edges of life. Uncle Clyde taught me how to relax with a little help from tobacco and bourbon or homemade wine. I especially appreciate Uncle Clyde's teachings about the opposite sex and relationships with the same. It probably wasn't an enlightened viewpoint, but it certainly has helped me get along.

Aunt Buehla cut my hair. Uncle Bob took me to a college campus and an Army Base (which I later signed up for both). Uncle Junior took me to a Cincinnati Reds game. Uncle Veachel took me deep sea fishing off the coast of North Carolina (I got sea sick so he recommended I only talk to the Army recruiter, the Navy was not going to be for me). Uncle Cecil took me to a horse race, a cattle auction and to a truck stop to order coffee and flirt with the waitress.

All in all, it was a pretty good mix. It taught me the value of hard work, sacrifice, and how to have fun without spending any money. Today we have Dr. Phil and psychologists making good money teaching us about self worth and how to reach deep inside to get by from day to day.

Maybe all these self help books, videos, and tapes could be replaced by studying the simple life on the farm. I am not talking about a mockery like MTV and Paris Hilton milking cows in designer gowns, I am talking about what my grandmother always said, "get after those chores" and the bible passage "as ye sow, so shall ye reap." She and they saw to it that I both sowed, and reaped.

ALMANAC

—▫—

The 2006 Old Farmer's Almanac is out and I had a chance to flip through the pages. Modern Almanacs contain more pages than the ones I remember from the 1950's and 60's. There are more advertisements in the modern Almanacs. The old ones had ads for Martha White Self Rising Flour and Watkins liniments and salves. The modern ads are for Gorilla Glue and Pheromones and male enhancements pills for increase in romance. My Grandmother would be turning over in her grave if she knew Almanacs had become a "dirty magazine" in her eyes.

Thank goodness, many of the useful charts are still in the new Almanac. I can see for Ohio the last frost will be May 3, 2006. That information will help me set out my tomato plants at just the right time. I always have a contest with the neighbors to see who has the first ripe tomato.

According to the charts, my Anniversary in August 2006 coincides with a full moon, which is good for love making. At my age, full moons don't occur often enough.

The Almanac's regional weather forecast is for us to have an exceptionally cold December and January, so I'd better cut some extra fire wood. I'll check my wool sock and long john underwear inventory as well. Having plenty of ice melt and a snow shovel that fits my wife's hands, is another item on my winter check list.

I can also tell by looking in the Almanac that my fishing trip planned for the middle of June 2006 will be a bust. The Almanac says that because of the position of the moon, the fish will not be biting. I had better plan on taking more beer and playing cards. Since we won't be catching fish, we may as well eat Limburger cheese and onion sandwiches on rye bread.

There is a lot of information for farmers in the Almanac. Dates are given for the best time to cut hay, breed livestock and when that is done, castrate animals. I don't butcher my own meat any more, but when we did, we didn't waste anything, including "those castrated parts." The Almanac also gives dates to plant beets, kale, musk melons, peas, sweet potatoes, and turnips, things my city slicker wife doesn't cook. She does look through the microwave recipes, which have been added down through the years.

My grandfather ordered lots of free catalogs from the Almanac. With no TV and only the monthly Life magazine to thumb thru, catalogs were our outside look at the world. We had catalogs from Ball Home Canning, Alden's Chicago Mail Order Co., Spiegel, Montgomery Ward, Belknap Hardware Co., Western Auto, Savage Fire Arms, Wayne Feeds, Allis-Chalmers Machinery and Equipment, Carnation Milk cooking, and the Deming Pump Company, just to name a few. We had our own reference library stacked in the broom closet. When the new catalogs came every year, the old catalogs were moved to the out house for recycling. The internet is just a digital collection of catalogs. We had our own, before Al Gore discovered computers linked together (remember Al took credit for starting the internet during his failed Presidential Campaign).

As a kid growing up on the farm, my favorite parts of the Almanac were the classified ads and the mind teasing games. The new Almanac has classified ads for seed companies, herbs, magnetic shoe inserts, and spiritual healers, pretty much the same as the Old Almanac. However, the new edition included phone numbers for singles looking for a mate, stay at home income schemes, cheap mortgages, and low cost prescription drugs.

I decided to try the mind teasing games on my city slicker wife. You try it too, see how well you do.

Which is larger, a bushel or a peck; a bale or a bundle; a rod or a furlong? She missed every question. How did you do?

ARE YOU A COUNTRY BOY?

—◻—

Jeff Foxworthy has made a good living producing CD's called, "You Know You're A Redneck If." My favorite is, "You know you're a redneck if you go to family reunions to look for women to date." We have a few rednecks in our family and most families do as well. I don't consider myself a redneck, but I do consider myself a country boy, and I bet many of you are as well. I have developed a little test to determine if you still qualify as a country boy. You know the old saying, "You can take the boy out of the country, but you can't take the country out of the boy."

If you see round steak on a restaurant menu and you think of a thick slice of fried bologna, you are still a country boy.

If you pass by a cattle feed lot and get a good whiff of the cow manure and the smell causes you to think of how much money the cattle will bring at the farm livestock auction, then you are still a country boy.

If something breaks on your truck or anywhere around home and the first thing you reach for in your tool box is baling wire, you are still a country boy.

If you smell fresh cut grass and it reminds you of putting up hay into the barn loft and the first time you made love in the hay loft, you are still a country boy.

If you are driving to work and a young rabbit darts out in front of your truck, is hit and thrown into the ditch, you are still a country boy if you think about getting some potatoes, onions and carrots and cooking some rabbit stew.

If you had you choice of dressing up and driving two hours, with a Dr. Phil tape playing, just to shop at a new Mall so you can buy things you don't need and have tea and quiche with your wife or, putting on a pair of overalls, Red Wing boots, a sweat stained ball cap, driving three miles to the Hardware Store, buying a ball of twine and shooting the breeze with other customers, if you choose the ball of twine over quiche, then you are still a country boy.

If you remember that the hard metal seat on the 9N Ford tractor was more comfortable than the cold leather seats on you wife's imported sedan, then you are still a country boy.

If you open the bill from the plumber for unclogging your toilet and installing a new garbage disposal and you think of how peaceful and Un-mechanical the old out house was back on the family farm and the fact that all those table scraps going down the garbage disposal could feed a lot of chickens, then you are still a country boy.

If the first cool Saturday morning in the fall your neighbor makes a fire in his fireplace and that whiff of wood smoke sets your thoughts, not on football, but on sharpening up the scrapers and knives and lubing up the sausage press because it's hog killing time, then you are still a country boy.

When driving to work half asleep one morning and

the radio disc jockey introduces a song by The Three Dog Night; you think he is giving a weather report saying it will be very cold tonight, then you are still a country boy. (For you city folks, the only time dogs are allowed in the farm house is when it was very cold outside and you need to protect the dogs and help keep you warm in bed…20 to 0 F, one dog, 0 - -20 F, two dogs, below -20 F requires three dogs in bed with you to make it thru the cold night).

APHRODISIACS

—⌐◻—

You can't turn on the TV today without viewing a pharmaceutical Ad about male erectile dysfunction. I get some what embarrassed when the ads come on a show my wife, daughter and I are watching. I remember watching the last Super Bowl. Seems every other commercial was some guy my age trying to throw a football through a moving tire swinging from a tree. I wonder if they are trying to send a Freudian message with the hole in the tire? Then another commercial follows showing a couple sitting buck naked in side by side claw foot bath tubs, outside over looking the ocean. Now how often does that happen? Next there is a baseball player who talks about hitting home runs with his Louisville Slugger baseball bat. Is this another scenario were the clever folks on Madison Avenue think they can put us in the mood to buy their products?

Finally, half time comes and I think to myself, no more sexual situations to embarrass me. Low and behold what happens … a wardrobe "accident"? Justin Timberlake pulls off one side of Janet Jackson's bra thereby exposing her right breast (or glob of silicone).

For the rest of the evening and the next few weeks, commentators were shocked by the incident. Congress and the Federal Communications Commission began holding hearings on how to prevent this suggestive type of behavior from being piped into our family living rooms. Give me a break. Are these the same politicians who take PAC money from the drug companies that are advertising the sex drugs? They are upset over one peek at a fake boob, while the country's national debt spirals out of control.

Back to sex drugs, they are not new. Aphrodisiacs have been around a long time. Oysters are said to add zip to your love life. This goes back to the Grand Duke of Russia who swallowed a dozen oysters and gave his love a pearl necklace. Did the oysters turn him on, or was it the necklace turning her on? History is not clear on this matter.

I tried the oyster thing once, when I was younger. I bellied up to the Union Oyster Bar in Boston. The Union Oyster Bar has a lot of history. Daniel Webster (of dictionary fame), who was a ladies man, used to swig pints of Ale and eat mollusks there. My friend Ken and I were on a company expense account so we swallowed a couple dozen raw oysters and washed them down with six or twelve draft beers. Then we headed out to the night life of Bean Town. I didn't get a change to see if the oysters worked. Too many beers and too much cocktail sauces caused me to turn in early. I do know this, regurgitated oysters, ketchup and beer sure didn't make me feel sexy.

My Uncle Clyde was... well my grandmother said he was a "ruffian." Uncle Clyde smoked, chewed, drank and ate about anything he thought would make for a good time or help him chaise women. Shrimp or crawdads are what Uncle Clyde ate before going out on the town. It made him feel "lucky." He bought Spanish Fly from "behind the counter" at the Drug Store to help his girlfriend feel lucky also. With a little aromatherapy (old spice shaving lotion) and a fifth of Uncle Jack Black (Jack Daniels Whiskey) Uncle Clyde was quite the ladies man.

Grandmother always had a bible quote that dealt with judgment day to emphasis her disapproval of a family member's behavior. To Uncle Clyde she quoted Luke 21:34, "Take heed to yourselves, lest your hearts be weighted down with carousing, drunkenness and cares of this life, and that day come on you unexpectedly."

Uncle Clyde was known to always have a comeback and he quoted the bible too. Ecclesiastes 8:15 "A man hath no better thing under the sun than to eat, and to drink, and be merry."

Grandmother would just shake her head.

CUT THE CHEESE PLEASE

—◻—

My daughter came home from college the other weekend to be with her parents. Well not really, she actually came home to visit with her friends, get a tank full of gas on mom and dad, and relieve us of a few groceries.

As she was checking her list prior to returning to OSU, she saw that she had forgotten cheese. She needed a particular type of cheese for making a dip for a margarita party. College kids today have theme parties. She had already raided our liquor cabinet for tequila and the fridge for Corona beer. Her mother had made her Mexican tortilla rolls and other Spanish hors d'oeuvres to take back. Before she returned to Columbus she wanted to pick up the cheese in Coshocton-so she doesn't have to use her own money.

I agreed to take her to the grocery because Cheese is something I know a little about.

Our family milked a few cows and sold the milk to a creamery that made Colby cheese. That cheese was great when melted over my grandmothers cracklin cornbread. Cheese and crackers were the main meal we ate whenever my family traveled. My father never stopped the car until we arrived at our destination. He packed a pound of sliced American cheese, some saltine crackers, and a carton of 8 ounce green glass coke-a-colas. That kept 4 boys in the back seat fed, and since my father would not stop the car, the empty 8 ounce bottles served as a personal urinal.

I refined my taste for cheese in the Army. I was stationed in a small town in Germany not far from the border with France. On one of the first NATO war scenarios I participated in, my unit shared a staging area with a French unit. The French soldiers were just like us, after evening roll call they too snuck away from their tents and went into town (that was off limits) looking for some action. The town we snuck into was nearly empty; all the young women had been herded away by their parents upon hearing a bunch of soldiers were in the region. As was often the case, we ended up in a bar and spent the evening sharing back home stories and drinking shooters, flaming shots and swigging Jagermeister.

We had ration cards that allowed us to buy cigarettes, hard liquor, and coffee really cheap at the Post Exchange (Marlboros 15 cents a pack.) The French soldiers had ration cards too. Their cards entitled them to buy good wine and fine cheese, cheap. French soldiers stationed outside of Europe also were rationed visits to a traveling bordello. Talk about ways to keep up morale. Anyway, when we got together with the French, we broke out the cartons of Marlboros and they brought out the Fromage. I learned a lot about Camberts, Brie, Chabichou du Poitou or Crayeux De Ronco. Their cheese had various textures from hard crumbly to runny, some were fragrant, others pungent, and still others were mixed with ham or sausage, or with herbs or vegetables. All French cheeses have rather romantic names which my French counter-parts schooled me in the European ways of using cheese in courting women. They told me to pack a picnic lunch consisting of a fine cheese, hard bread, and the appropriate wine. Take your date, a blanket and find a private spot along the river bank. I used this technique many times once the Army maneuvers were over and the parents allowed their daughters to return home.

Back to buying cheese with my daughter. We get to the dairy section of the grocery and she picked out a cheese whiz to make her Mexican dip. I read the label and told her I bet this stuff never saw a cow. I don't buy cheese at a grocery, I began to pontificate. I buy real cheese at Randles Cheese House, The Cheesery in Roscoe or at Pearl Valley Cheese. I began pointing out to my daughter that real cheese is not sold in aerosol cans like spray paint, is not sold in tubes like painters caulk, is not sold in tubs that you later use to clean paint brushes, is not sold in little slices with plastic wrap between each slice, is not precut into little bite sized cubes and packed in zip lock bags and real cheese is never sold in a jar with easy off lids. By now other shoppers were looking at us.

My daughter said, "Dad that's enough, I can't take you anywhere."

TELEMARKETING

—▫—

I guess I am not on the new federal "Don't Call List", because the other evening I got a telemarketing call. The young lady explained to me how stupid I was by staying with my current phone service. She spoke of free minutes and roll overs. She even mentioned paying me money (which Yogi says is just as good as cash) to switch carriers.

Oh, how I long for the old days when we didn't have choices. We had only one Phone Company then, a good old fashion monopoly. We didn't have any free time minutes, no 10-10-220, or other magic number to memorize for making long distance calls. We did not have a rate for calling Canada, no European weekend rates either. We never called outside the county back then anyway. No 800 or 900 numbers either. Roaming was not a phone term back then, it was used to describe what we did on Saturday night, looking for some action.

Our phone was a table model and it came in only one color, black. Everyone's phone was black. We didn't own the phone, it was owned by the almighty phone company. You did not install your own phones then either. If you moved, you called the phone company and begged them to hook up the four little wires that connected you to the grid. The phone company would then tell you they would be by between 8:00 a.m. and 4:00 p.m. Monday through Friday the third week of next month and you must be home for the phone man to perform this highly technical feat. It was understood they were in charge and you were lucky if they would even let you use their phones.

We were on a party line. There were sixteen other homes connected to our line. We each had a distinctive ring to notify us that we had a call. Our ring sounded like all the other fifteen distinctive rings when you were on the front porch and a call came in. Normally at least four other people answered our ring. Mean widow Miss Ollie could always be counted on answering; using the excuse that her hearing aid was going bad and she could not tell what ring she heard. Uncle Clyde said she was just "nosey". The phone numbers back then were only three digits, ours was 331. Our neighbor Billy Joe Richardson was always dialing our number when he called home from the pool hall to tell his mother he was having car trouble and would be late for supper. Seems Billy Joe's ability to remember his phone number decreased with the amount of long necks he had at Aunt Nora's Pool Hall.

Bobby Ray and I acquired a "phone" from Uncle Clyde, whose waitress friend got it from a truck driver who worked for the L & N Railroad. We rigged up the wiring by taping into the line out side the farm house. We ran the wires out to the smokehouse, which served as our club house when it rained. We never got up the nerve to call out on the phone, however. We were afraid someone from the phone company would be able to trace the line and they would send a phone truck full of linemen to eliminate us. I didn't want my grandmother to bear the shame of having her grandson arrested by the phone police.

However, we did listen in once in a while to others using the party line. And guess what, old mean widow Miss Ollie had a beau. I heard him once ask her to a movie. Uncle Clyde said the guy must be blind to ask out that ugly a woman. Bobby Ray and I listen in on Uncle Clyde's phone calls to his waitress friends once in a while. That was like dialing a 900 number today. We sure got our ears full.

WEDDINGS

—⊡—

I see that General Motors is re-introducing a 60's muscle car, the GTO. Wait a minute, do you remember those cars from our youth? Those cars with the four speed on the floor? You know what happens with four on the floor? You couldn't make out in the front seat, so you and your girl got in the back seat. I had a cousin, Ezra who had a 1961 Chevy Impala Super Sport 2 door hard top, white with red interior, four on the floor, dual Quads, and posi-traction.

He got his high school sweet heart pregnant and had to get married. Uncle Cecil and his boy Ezra were big time corn farmers.

Everything they owned in the way of clothing was either John Deere Green with the Deere or Pioneer Seed Corn logo.

When Ezra got married he had just returned from a trip to Kansas City on a FFA Convention. Ezra bought brand new blue corduroy FFA Jackets for himself and his bride to be. They decided to get married in their FFA Jackets. Instead of throwing rice as the couple departed the church we threw kernels of Pioneer hybrid corn. Uncle Clyde said that made good sense. Bobby Ray and I had to pick up the kernels and take them to our chickens. Grandmother said, "Waste not, want not."

The reception was held at Uncle Cecil's house with cake and Neapolitan ice cream. When it came time to toss the garter belt there was none. They forgot. My cousin, Carol Lynn went to the corn crib and got an ear of Pioneer seed corn in the husk. They pulled the husk back and tied the silk with a string (like city slickers do today when they hang fall decorations on their front door).

When Ezra's bride threw the corn over her shoulder to the young maidens, their old mongrel dog Pioneer (I told you Ezra loved this corn growing thing), Pioneer thought it was a pitch and fetch game. Pioneer snatched the corn out of the air before anyone had a chance. Pioneer took off with his catch and ran around the yard with all the kids chasing him.

Ezra and his bride had to be in school Monday so they did not take a week off for a honeymoon. We all took a week when it was tobacco planting time, tobacco cutting time, and a few days here and there to plant or combine corn, but taking off from high school just to have a honeymoon was never done. Instead, Ezra and his bride drove to Nashville that evening to attend the Grand Ole Opry in Ryman Auditorium. They still had their wedding attire, FFA jackets on. After the Opry they tried to buy some cocktails at one of the piano lounges on Printer's Alley, but got ID'ed and were refused service.

Even today you can get married at any age, but you must be mature (21) to buy a cocktail.

Anyway, Ezra drove to a Holiday Inn on the edge of town and checked into a room to celebrate the beginning of marital bliss.

That's not the end of the story. Ezra graduated from high school, joined the Army, did a tour in "Nam", returned home and kept making babies and Pioneer corn.

Today he farms about a thousand acres of corn and a few acres of tobacco, a big garden, hogs and beef, and of course hens for fresh eggs.

To this day, if you stop by his farm while he is doing chores he either has on his FFA jacket or his Army fatigue jacket (they both still fit him).

So, to you young brides planning to spend your parent's retirement money for a fancy wedding complete with all the hooplah, just have a simple wedding and throw corn.

As Uncle Clyde would probably say, "Don't spend a fortune on weddings, do it for chicken feed".

THE END OF THE WORLD IS NEAR

My grandmother was a devote bible toter. She never went anywhere without it and she quoted it often. The Revelations of John was a book of visions that only the faithful could understand. Grandmother could pick out current happenings and find an apocalyptic meaning. Grandmother believed that Satan's final defeat at Armageddon could be forecasted by mapping Revelations on to present day events.

I remember when the Russians put the first satellite in space. Sputnik, she felt was a sign telling us the end of the world was at hand and she would stress the urgency to Christianization to my Uncle Clyde, who had brown bottle fever (also called longneck beer ailment).

Grandmother predicted the second coming of Christ based on ecclesiastical warnings of harlots of Babylon, when one of my city cousins showed up at a family reunion wearing a mini skirt, go-go boots, sporting a bouffant hair do and showing everyone her round case containing birth control pills.

Long haired naked hippies swimming in a pond during the epic Woodstock Music Festival made the front page of our home town newspaper. Grandmother equated their lascivious manner to the prophecy of the beast from the sea.

When Gloria Steinman started the National Organization of Women and thus began the Women's Lib Movement, grandmother predicted that Satan had a hand in wife's rebelling against their husbands and the second coming of Christ was near.

The Surgeon General determined that smoking was a health hazard in 1965 and required cigarette manufactures to place warnings on all packs. Grandmother saw this as a sign from Revelations that the government was Antichrist and proclaiming itself as the Messiah. She felt the government would soon add snuff to its list of evil products. To a tobacco farmer's wife who dipped snuff until she died at age 90, the government's actions would have required Christ to come back to earth and right this wrong.

My father made the mistake of bringing grandmother along to pick me up at a school dance in 1964. They arrived before the dance was over and she saw with her own two eyes teenagers dancing the twist, mashed potato, swim, and the watusi. My father had to get out the smelling salts to keep her from fainting. On the way home she spoke of prophecy saying Satan would invade people's bodies and they would shake uncontrollably.

Although Grandmother's Apocalyptic signs never come to pass, I have learned of an event that I am sure is a sign the world is coming to an end.

Associated Press 9-24-2004

SACRAMENTO, Calif. - California yesterday became the first state to ban weeding by hand on most farms, saying the work is too backbreaking for laborers. Under a rule approved by the California Occupational

Safety and Health Division, farm workers, in most cases, will not have to stoop to pull weeds, but instead will be given long-handled tools that will allow them to work without bending over. The rule takes effect within two weeks.

Now I have used a long handle device (a hoe) to weed many a row in our garden next to the farm house, but you can't properly weed a garden without getting down on all fours and pulling weeds with the two hands God gave us. To have a government enmity (Satan) to tell us not to pull weeds is a sure sign the end of the world is at hand.

THE FOXHOLE

—◻—

Coshocton recently played host to a bicycle stage race, part of the Tour of Ohio, professional cycling circuit.

These young male bike racers hailed from all over our grand lands, Boston, Anarbor, Austin, Chicago, Atlanta, Columbus, D.C. just to name a few. Then there were a few riders from down under, Sydney and Auckland. As the riders gather for the start of the fifty mile race, the race director covered some safety issues and some danger points. Although riding out state route 541, then turning north onto route 79 toward the highest point in Coshocton County, New Castle is not the same as the twist and turns of the switch backs accenting the Alps leading up to the Alpe d' Huez during le Tour de Frances; there are some challenges none the less. The director was pointing out some of the hair pin turns, when one of the Aussie raised his hand for a question. "Yes" said the race director. "Will the route go by the Foxhole", the Kid from Sydney inquired?

Now why is it some young man from ten thousand miles away, who has been in our town all of thirty minutes already knows about a strip club in the middle of nowhere? As I was discussing the cycling race and the route with my colleges at work the next day, one asked, did they ride by the Foxhole?

Why is it that young men only have one thing on

their minds?

I asked Dave if he had any strip joint experiences

Dave asked me if I had ever been to a strip tease joint? My grandmother would be rolling in her grave if she knew, but yes once when I was in the Army. My buddy, Bernie and I got a three day pass and we took a bus to Paris, the city of lights. As we approached the Effille Tower, I was spellbound. The tallest thing I ever saw growing up on the farm was Mr. Bales silo. We passed by the museum the, Louvre were Leonardo DaVincis painting the Mona Lisa hangs. Up the Avenue de Champs Elysées and around the Arc de Triomphe we traveled to our hotel. Our Hotels concierges immediately recognized us as American GI's because we had very short hair. He gave us a map of the subway and told us of a couple of places in Pigalle (the red light district).

We took our concierges advise and patronized the Le Tiger. The maître d' took us to a table past a cage with a go go dancer inside and he said a couple of young french ladies would like to join us for some champaign. "Sure" we said, and the girls pulled up a chair. We drained the bottle in no time, the girls said they had to go to the ladies room, but they would like some more champaign.

"Wow, I think they like us, I said to Bernie. Yea, hey Tom lets get two bottles." About then the maître d' comes by for our order and ask us to pay the check for the first bottle. I looked at the bill, 455.00 French Francs (around $110.00). Bernie said, lets get out of here, we have been had. We each threw a Fifty Franc bill on the table and headed for the door. The maître d' was following us yelling something about calling the Gendarmerie (police). We returned to our room and just watch French television, which was showed more skin than we saw with our one hundred dollar experience.

BURMA SHAVE

—▣—

A friend of mine bought a new van recently and it contains a TV so the kids can watch DVD's while they travel. He felt this was a good feature to control his children in the back seat. I feel sorry for people who have to "control" their kids.

Travel in the 1950's in the family station wagon was not controlled, it was spontaneous. There was so much to see in traveling the two lane highways and byways there was no time for boredom.

There were road signs of all sizes, shapes, and colors for us to read and learn about the area we were traveling through. There were no National Franchise Restaurants, Hotels and Amusements Parks then, hawking their wares with Madison Ave. city slicker billboards. Every area had its local flavor and it was called to our attention by signs made by local sign makers who had their own unique style.

We lost a lot in the late 1960's when the First Lady, Lady Byrd Johnson, championed her Highway Beautification Act. Lady Byrd's legislation withheld federal highway dollars, if the states allowed bill boards and signs along the right of ways. Her intention was to clean up some of the trashy areas in certain sections of most towns. It is somewhat ironic that Lady Byrd was the ugliest woman ever to live in the White House. My Uncle Clyde said it was appropriate that her name was Byrd,

31

because her nose looked like the beak of a chicken hawk. We had an ugly woman telling us how to make our highways beautiful.

The effect of Lady Byrd's law backfired. All the local signs that were funny and enlightening had to be taken down, but they were replaced by huge billboards, set back the legal 200 yards off the highway. Mom and Pop businesses could not afford these humongous signs. Instead, large oil companies with their truck stop signs, chains of adult book stores, and TV News personalities are plastered against the former pastures and woodlands. These large, gaudy, tacky, ugly signs have ruined the country side.

Not too long ago highway signs were small and were only on the final approach to our cities and villages. There was Chew Mail Pouch Tobacco painted on barns, and Dun Rovin Café signs leading into West Lafayette calling out to travelers looking for good home style country cooking. The Tourraine Club was announced before Newcomerstown and The Close Inn and The Olde Town Drive In before Coshocton. Marsh Wheeling Cigars signs called out to us to light up and relax with a Stogie.

Many companies had traveling salesmen who would gladly give lots of free tin signs advertising their products to country stores and feed mills. These signs made their way to barns and served as another building material to cover holes in walls and floors. A side benefit was these signs added a little artistic class to the milking parlor at 4:00 o'clock in the morning. Martha White Self

Rising Flour and Bull Durham smoking tobacco are the ones I remember the most.

Where I grew up, the most read signs were Burma Shave. Burma Shave Signs were used not only to entice passersby to shave with this new fangled foamy soap, but their signs were used to teach kids how to read and spell. They were like parables in the bible. Here are some classics.

Passing School Zone
Take it Slow
Let our Little
Shavers Grow
Buy Burma Shave

The Midnight Ride
Of Paul for Beer
Led to a
Warmer Hemisphere
Burma Shave

Let's Make Hitler
And Hirohito
Look as sick as
Old Benito
Buy defense Bonds
Burma-Shave

Maybe you can't
Shoulder a gun
But you can shoulder
The cost of one
Buy defense bonds
Burma-Shave

———◆◆———

Don't pass cars
On curve or hill
If the cops
Don't get you
Morticians will
Burma-Shave

———◆◆———

Does your husband
Misbehave
Grunt and grumble
Rant and rave
Shoot the brute some
Burma-Shave

Reading signs, playing I Spy, looking for out of state car license plates, boy traveling was fun back then. No DVD required.

STUBBORN AS A MULE

As those who have read this column in the past will note, I mostly observe the ironies in life. I try to compare these little situations of modern life with our methods of handling things on the farm.

While watching the cable news, I have observed that most of the folks involved in the celebrity court news are disembarking from a stretch limousine or a custom Hummer They leap out to the howls of the newshounds and the flash of the photographers' bulbs. It was different down home.

Down home, the courthouse was a good place to whittle, play checkers, and listen to the opinions of the men there. They held court with few penalties but many opinions. Now that I think of it, it was a lot like the Fair View General Store, except dogs weren't allowed and you couldn't buy Mail Pouch.

There really wasn't much to see at the courthouse. There weren't any stock scandals, and no one had heard of Enron, Martha Stewart, market manipulation or insider trading. Uncle Clyde tried to corner the market in contraband sippin' whiskey, but never succeeded. There weren't any insiders to trade; we just hoped the tobacco allotment check would cover the charges at the general store. We didn't worry about court issues, let alone transportation to the courthouse.

Our transportation was an old pickup or Bill and Betsy, our mules. It made me ponder if we used mules today, how would it change things? I think it would not only lighten the judicial load but also help cure recidivism. No one would willingly abuse the court system if they had to show up on a mule. The spectacle alone would have a deterrent effect, and dealing with a mule for a few hours might equal a month in solitary. While Bill and Betsy were the core of the farm, they brought to life the expression "Stubborn as Mules". When Bill and Betsy felt they had done enough for the day, they stopped. Dynamite would not move them.

Later, in the Army, I was stationed in Colorado. The transient quarters were in the "Mule Barns". The barns were as gloriously appointed as the name implies. I was just glad they had moved the mules out before they moved me in.

Somehow, if Martha had to arrive on a mule, I don't think we'd be seeing nearly as much as we do. That's a good thing, too.

CHRISTMAS GIFTS

—⊡—

As I have written previously, many of the traditions of Christmas past have been lost due to the recommendations of some consultant with an M.B.A.

As I look over the pile of gifts under our Christmas tree, I can't help but think how much money some M.B.A. is making by hyping up some techno gadget that makes an easier job of a task I don't want to do anyway. At my age, I don't really need anything except air and nourishment. However, TV ads make a compelling case for my loved one to buy me the latest tool I don't need.

This year the M.B.A.'s took space age laser technology and incorporated into a "straight line laser level". This Forty Dollar must have tool performs the same function as a free wooden yard stick and a five dollar level. By purchasing this new tool, the M.B.A.'s using new math figures this gift will fuel the third quarter growth of our nation's G.D.P. Using my arithmetic, I figure my loved one just wasted forty bucks.

This laser level supposedly makes easy work of such tasks as wall papering and hanging pictures. My grandmother taught me to hang wall paper and ceiling paper using wheat paste, a yardstick and a plumb bob. I'm sure she would laugh herself silly watching someone today trying to hang today's pre-pasted paper using one of these laser levels. There was not a square corner in any of the rooms in our farm house, so the laser level would probably only have been used to torment one of our cats. The laser level TV commercials also show how easy it is to plan and hang new closet organizers. We didn't have closets in our farm house. We stored items on the steps leading to the attic and in the attic itself. The attic was big enough that you didn't have to organize things. We just piled things along the eaves, making sure we didn't block access to the quilting frame that hung in the middle of the room. On days we couldn't work in the fields because of rain, we would tinker around in the attic and then take a nap. You haven't experienced true deep sleep until you have taken a nap with a summer rain beating against the attic's tin roof.

Another feature of this must have tool is that it was made in China. This means about the only Americans benefiting from selling this tool is the longshoremen who unload the boat and of course the M.B.A.'s marketing things we don't need. All my gifts this year were manufactured in some third world country. I was given a ball cap made in Vietnam this year. When I was going through Army boot camp the summer of 1969, I sure never envisioned getting anything made in Vietnam, ever.

I long for Christmas of my youth. Back then we received one toy, some clothing, candy, nuts, and fruit. Everything was made in America then, except the oranges from Florida. For some reason my grandfather thought Florida was still a foreign country, a Seminole Indian nation. Uncle Clyde knew better. Uncle Clyde had been to Florida once. He said folks down there wore shorts and sandals. He also said a lot of wealthy folks from Chicago spent their winters in Florida. "You could tell who the snow birds were, he said, because they wore socks with their sandals."

All our toys were made from metal back then, no plastic. I guess plastic had not been discovered yet. That would come along later after Dustin Hoffman made the movie "The Graduate".

All our clothing gifts were made in America too. About the only thing I ever remember getting that was made in the Far East was Chinese checkers. Now that I think about it, those Chinese checkers were about as useless as my new laser level.

Summertime is Camp Time

—▱—

I enjoyed a relaxing evening at the recent Phil Dirt and the Dozier's concert held at the Coshocton County Fair Grounds.

It was an evening to reminisce and enjoy the great groups from the 50's.

After returning to my house for refreshments, the conversation centered on what our kids and grandkids were doing for the summer. One friend said the summer is not long enough for her grandson to fit in all the camps he wants to attend.

Soccer Camp, Boy Scout Camp, Space Camp and Zoo Camp were top on this grandson's list, but he also wanted to attend Basketball Camp, Inventors Camp, Swim Camp, 4-H Camp, Band Camp, Vacation Bible School (VBS) and especially Gymnastics Camp because it is held at the same facility that is hosting a Cheer Leaders Camp.

Others had grandkids participating in yet other Summer Camps. I had never heard of Leadership, International Horsemanship, and Lacrosse…..

Then the conversation turned to camps we Baby Boomers attended.

There were lots of Camp Ohio attendees in our little group of "Boomers" and a few Band Campers, and it seemed all went to VBS. I tried to avoid any participation in this stroll down memory lane by refreshing everyone's drinks. However, my turn came when I was asked what camps farm boys went to in the summer.

Keep in mind my guests were all city slickers so I thought what the heck, I'll make up some camps. City Folks are too busy being busy; it will just go over their heads.

"The first camp of the year was in April, Tobacco Bed Planting Camp", I boasted. I wasn't going to be out camped by these city folks.

"Next came Gardening Camp, then Hoeing Camp. Mid-summer was Clean the Barn Camp. My favorite was Blackberry Picking Camp, followed by Shooting Ground Hog Camp. Bean Picking and Shelling Camp lead directly into Pickling and Canning Camp without so much as week-end break." I said. "I even got out of School a few days in the fall for Butchering and Hog rendering camp."

By now my wife had figured out that I was being a smart ass. Other guests got a little chuckle, but one unsuspecting boomer who grew up in the suburbs stated, "Wow, I bet all those camp fees really added up to a lot of money!"

I told him that the fees were offset by the room and board grant. I don't think he understood.

TREES

—⬚—

Spring makes me feel good. It seems that as the days grow longer and warmer and the sap starts up the trees, I too feel my body juices flowing again. I feel that it's time to tune up my bike and get after it again. I've been riding since I was five, and it just makes me feel like it's spring again.

Back to spring and trees. We all had favorite trees when we were growing up. One of my favorite was the big beech tree by our farm house. The beech had very smooth bark. With a sharp barlow knife I could carve my initials and those of my heart throb at the time. That beech had generations of initials and poems written on it. I bet some Archaeologist will come along some day and compare our carvings to the hieroglyphics found in King Tuts Tomb.

We had a black walnut tree in the beef cattle pasture that was like a drug store to my grand mother. Any type of skin rash was treated with the juice from the bark or husk of the nut.

Sassafras saplings made excellent fishing poles, and the roots were boiled for another of grandmothers teas to treat stomach ailments. A weeping willow tree by the pond had limbs flexible enough to use as tying material for building play forts out of tomato stakes and locust fence posts. The high limbs of the white oak trees that grew out over the creek bank had wild grape vines growing in them. Once cut, we could swing on the vines and make jungle noises like Tarzan.

The trees in our orchard were a ready source for switches for whipping my young butt for doing things I was told not to do, but did anyway, like cutting Sunday school, smoking, sipping Uncle Clyde's home made wine, or skinny dipping. This list could get very lengthy.

The mulberry tree was the most fun tree. When school was out, my city cousins always made a trip to the farm. On more than one occasion I watched my older cousin park his white 1955 Ford Victoria under that mulberry tree. The first of June is when that tree yielded up thousands of plumb purple berries, that when eaten by the pigeons and black birds made a vivid violet colored bird poop that really showed up on that white car hood.

Along the back field fence row was a grove of hickory nut and persimmon trees (technically persimmons grow on a bush). I was the hunting guide come squirrel season. I always took my city cousins to these hickory nut trees to find and shoot squirrels. I was good at calling the game and every one bagged their limit. I was also good at getting an unsuspecting cousin to sample a green persimmon. In October after the persimmons were ripened by the first frost, they were uniquely sweet and fruity. A green persimmon in September at the start of the hunting season can pucker your mouth so bad that you think your taste buds will never recover. Add the green persimmon scheme to the list of reasons I had to cut my own switch off one of the trees in our orchard.

I miss the trees on our family farm. I had a sugar maple tree in my last yard. It produced thousands of those winged seeds in the spring that float down like little helicopters to land all over my neighbors' deck, porch and driveway, and plugged up their gutters and down spouts. I should have cut that tree down, but like the mulberry tree, it served a purpose (to aggravate folks who get excited over nothing). If my grandmother were alive, I would be going to the orchard to cut a switch for making that comment.

YOU'NS AND YA'LL

—⊡—

I love Ohio. Though it is not Kentucky, I have grown to love the diverse nature, and mostly unspoiled beauty of the state. Rural Ohio reminds me a lot of rural Kentucky, my homeland. There are beautiful hills, the bountiful lakes, and the good people just like home. I was concerned that things would be very different.

When I first moved to Ohio from the south, I didn't notice much difference. Country folk are country folk, regardless of which side of the Mason Dixon Line they grew up on. "Did you get a deer, how about that #3 car at Daytona and did you see that dress Dolly Parton wore at the Country Music Awards?" are common themes to start a conversation, whether you hail from Coshocton or Nashville.

Instead of hunting for tender Poke Greens in the spring, we hunt mushrooms around here. Instead of addressing people with Ya'll, we use You'ns around here. Instead of Grits for breakfast, we eat home fries around here. Instead of Fall City or Sterling Beer, we drink Bud or Miller around here. But other than those few differences, Coshocton is like any small town down South.

Now just drive a hundred miles north of Coshocton and you are smack dab in the middle of "Yankee Country". Those folks are different and they talk funny. If I had to pick a person that exemplifies Cleveland, it would be Dennis Kucinich. Dennis is of Eastern European Heritage, talks a lot and fast too and he thinks he know everything. He is the kind of fellow my Uncle Clyde would like to buy for what he is worth and sell him for what he thinks he is worth.

For those who have forgotten, Dennis was the Boy Mayor of Cleveland at one time. He led the City into a financial default and the Cuyahoga River was so polluted, it caught on fire when he was mayor. He recently ran for the Democratic Presidential Nomination, finishing eleventh in a field of twelve. Some say he was only campaigning so he could meet women and find that perfect mate to make wife #4.

I am not saying everyone from Cleveland is short, has funny ears, and a loud mouth. I know lots of folks who have moved from Cleveland down to

God's Country (Coshocton County) and adjusted right in to our slower pace and way of life.

Uncle Clyde always claimed there were three types of Yankees. There were the folks that circumstances placed in the North, they were Yankees. Then there were the folks who came into Bluegrass Country for a visit or a taste of the good life, they were damn Yankees. Then there were a few souls who stayed, they were - - - damn Yankees. Even here, there are some that move down here that will always be Yankees and just because they buy a little hunting cabin along one of Coshocton County's unpolluted rivers, they are still damn Yankees.

You can spot these damn Yankees a mile away. The damn Yankee men in the summer time wear shorts and sandals with socks. All normal folks know sandals are to be worn with bare feet. They are convinced they are land barons because they own two acres and a Coleman trailer along the river. During deer season, these Yankees buy a thousand dollar shot gun and cheap whiskey and try to hunt when they are three sheets to the wind.

Yankee women, wear too much perfume, have lots of rings on their fingers, gold chains around their necks, and pop their chewing gum (even in their sleep I am told), sort of Brooklynites without the sophistication. Their hair is held high on their head with several cans of hair spray, and they wear go-go boots, even though they went out of style, 30 years ago.

Uncle Clyde would have just shaken his head.

APRÉS – SKI

—▢—

I was watching a TV show the other night about the rich and famous skiing at St. Moritz Switzerland. I had the opportunity to spend a weekend skiing on the slopes of St. Moritz once when I was in the U.S. Army stationed in Europe. I rubbed elbows and butted in on the lift line with some celebrities and royalty. I dined on Kase Fondue and shots of Kirch Waser (cherry schnapps) at an après-ski (after ski) party. I had great fun skiing with my German and Swiss friends, but winter sports on the farm were just as much fun.

We didn't have any mountain peaks as high as the Alps on our farm, but we had a couple of pretty steep knobs. When I was small, Bobby Ray and I would use a #14 Aluminum Grain Scoop as a sled. Just put your butt in the shovel and grab the handle and let gravity do the rest. The handle could be maneuvered so we didn't hit any tree stumps. When we were older, we procured an old car hood and used it as a sled. As I remember the 1948 Mercury had a large hood ornament that acted as a keel. That allowed the hood to descend in a straight line. The only problem was there were no brakes.

At the bottom of our sled run, flowed Goose Creek. We attempted to stop the hood before splashing into the creek by putting our legs outside the hood and dragging our feet in the snow. If we couldn't stop in time and took a dip in the creek, we ran to the smoke house to change into dry clothes. My friend Dave said that kids in Coshocton used an enameled bed pan from the Moore Enameling Company as a down hill racer.

If we had an Ice Storm, we hooked a log chain up to the three point hitch on Billy Joe Richardson's Farmall Tractor. At the end of the chain we attached a tree from the mule's rigs. We strapped on to our boots Oak slats from a tobacco packing basket. The slats were curved on the end like a real ski. Little did I know that the tobacco baskets were probably made in Dresden, Ohio by Dave Longaberger's father. We grabbed hold of the mule tree and were pulled along the icy lane by the Farmall.

An afternoon of hooding and towing caused us to work up an appetite and thirst. We brought up a jar of pickled bologna and pickled eggs from the cellar to warm our bones. For dessert we had snow ice cream.

Snow Ice Cream = scoops of freshly fallen fluff snow, vanilla extract, sugar, stir and eat with a spoon from a cup. Most of the snow on the farm was pristine, no pollution in the air to foul the snow as it falls from the sky. The only thing we had to watch out for was the Yellow Snow. Yellow snow could be caused by our dog Blackie urinating in the snow, or by Uncle Clyde being too lazy to walk the entire length of the path to the outhouse. My friend Dave, who grew up on 6th St., in Coshocton says they could not make Snow Ice Cream in his neighborhood because everyone had a coal furnace. A coal furnace is great on a three dog night, but the soot the furnace gives off turns the freshly fallen snow into a grey carpet. Now my father and Uncle Clyde always added a little bourbon to their snow ice cream. Their reasoning was that since the Russians had put up Sputnik, you never knew what was in the air; hence the bourbon could act as an antiseptic to kill off any unseen organisms in the air. Yes sir, bourbon was our miracle drug on the farm.

HOMOGENIZED AMERICA

—◫—

The first job I ever got paid for was when I was five years old. I don't remember all the details myself, but in my grandmother's later years it became one of her favorite stories. I was paid 25 cents for helping the farmer across the lane from our farm, Mr. Richardson put up hay. Uncle Clyde would put the International 1 ton truck in first gear, let out on the clutch, and set idle slow enough that the flat bed truck inched along, allowing the field hands to load bales of hay. My job was to stand on the driver's seat and steer the truck straight. Ironically, my grandmother didn't reminisce about my driving at age 5, but about lunch.

The owner of the farm fed the field hands at dinner time (lunch). While the men had Baptist Beer (Ice Tea) with their meal, I had milk. This is where my grandmother's story starts. Farmers then served whole milk, un-pasteurized, not homogenized. I was so fond of the milk from Mr. Richardson's cows that when the hay was all in the barn loft and the day's work done, I did not want to go home! I wanted to stay with the Richardson's because their milk was better than our milk. It was like I put myself up for adoption, hoping I would be fed this sweeter milk.

I later learned that Mr. Richardson's cows were Brown Swiss and he fed them good alfalfa hay and silage, plus his pastures were sown in Timothy and Orchard grass. Our farm had a few Holstein cows that grazed on fescue and wild onions. Our milk was sold to a creamery to make cheese and Mr. Richardson modern equipment and his milk was sold to a dairy.

My grandmother's story continued on to the next year when I started the 1st grade. It seems the teacher sent a note home after the 1st week that I would not drink my school milk. I wouldn't drink it because it was packed in paper cartons with a wax coating, making the milk taste like wax too. Grandmother agreed that store bought, pasteurized, homogenized milk does not taste right. It's not real milk, I said.

As I grow older, a lot of things lose their uniqueness. Things become homogenized.

When I was stationed in the Army at Ft. Carson, Colorado, every time I went home to visit, everyone wanted me to bring some Coors Beer. Coors was not sold east of the Mississippi River. It was unique and everyone wanted it because, well, because the Midwest and East Coast wasn't suppose to have Coors. Now Coors is just another beer.

When I did a brief tour of duty in North Carolina, everyone back home wanted me to bring them Krispy Cream Donuts. Krispy Creams were unique and folks wanted them North of the Ohio River because, well because they were not suppose to have them. Now Krispy Creams are everywhere and they have lost their appeal.

Interstate Highways have helped homogenize America. In the 50's travel on highways like Rt. 40 or 31 was fun. All roads went through downtowns main streets, past court houses. We stopped and ate in family restaurants. We got information from gas attendants working the Gulf, Texaco, Sinclair, or Sunoco gas stations. While the attendant was checking our fluid levels, washing the windshield and checking the tire pressure, they would give us weather forecasts and local attractions. No need for radar detectors then either, the gas attendant knew where the speed traps were and he would share that with you, if you gave a little gratuity.

We traveled back then mainly to visit friends and family. In the 50's we did not waste a whole day to travel on interstates (that all look alike), to an outlet mall (that all have the same stores) to shop for things we don't need (that is all made in China) and eat in a Restaurant Chain (that all have dirty bathrooms) and drink homogenized milk. I miss real milk.

You Can't Go Home Again!

—◫—

I had the occasion to visit the family farm recently. I had not been back for 20 years, ever since we had the auction. The night before my trip, I had dreams of my youth on the farm. I dreamed of the barn, its tin roof and rough sawn native oak plank boards. I dreamed of the first time in the hay loft, when Carolyn Lynn and I played Doctor and Nurse.

I dreamed of the pond just outside the barn. I shot frogs and turtles with my 22 rifle in that pond. I also did a lot of skinny dipping in that pond, at first with my cousin Bobby Ray and then with several local girls who were uninhibited enough to cool off on a hot summer day. After all, we didn't have air conditioning in those days.

There was the machinery shed attached to the barn. I worked on my first car there, a 1956 Chevy. My buddies were buying muscle cars, GTO's, Super Sports, 442's and the like, all with bucket seats and 4 on the floor. Uncle Clyde helped me pick out my "56" with a 6 banger, 3 speed on the column and bench seats (better for dating and making out.)

I dreamed of the outhouse behind the chicken coop and how peaceful it was to sit in there as long as a breeze blew from the west. If the wend blew from the west, I could smell the hams hanging in the smoke house. I pictured the big front porch, full of rocking chairs and a stool with a checker game awaiting play after supper.

Then my dreams ran through our big farm house, from the root cellar all the way to the attic, chasing one of my three little brothers who had gotten into my butch wax I used to hold my flat top haircut up.

I had butterflies in my stomach as I turned off the main road onto our lane we shared with about 10 other farms. As I approached the 1st farm house, where Bobby Ray grew up, I noticed about a half dozen kids in the front yard playing with a homemade swing hanging from a big oak tree. The kids smiled and waved. They looked a little grubby, but it was Saturday afternoon, perhaps they hadn't had their Saturday night bath yet. In fact they looked like me and my cousins when we were 5 or 6, except they all wore straw hats. I noticed the farm had horses in the field, clothes on the line out back, and a windmill. The fence rows were clean, fence posts straight, and wire tight. There was a big garden, a dog running loose, and lots of cats. I thought I was having a flash back! Then it dawned on me. Amish were farming Bobby Ray's old farm.

Then the next farm had a newly built house, well kept land, and kids every where. It too was Amish. In fact the next 4 farms were all about as I had remembered and they were all Amish.

As I passed the stand of white oaks that marked the start of our old homestead, things changed. The fence rows were grown up with weeds. The barn was gone, replaced with a metal pole building. The pond was filled in. There were no more out buildings. The farm house did not seem as big, maybe because there was no longer a porch. Gone too, was the big beech tree in the front yard where my father carved his initials inside of a heart and I carved my initials at the end of an arrow with CLM (Carolyn Lynn Martin) at the pointed end. The lawn was not groomed the way it was when I cut the grass with our reel push mower. There was a blow up wading pool in the front yard and a couple of kids who didn't wave. Instead of Uncle Clyde's 9N Ford Tractor in the driveway, there was now a pickup with huge wheels (monster truck). Rednecks now own what once was a working farm. That was enough, I sped away. I hope if I return in another 20 years, the Amish will have taken over the old homestead and made it a real farm again.

THERE IS DANGER IN THAT
PEANUT BRITTLE

—▣—

I love Halloween, not just because our hardware store sells a lot of mailboxes around Trick or Treat day. I love Halloween because I remember

we would go pick out a pumpkin out of our garden and make a jack-o-lantern, using our own imagination and my grandmother's favorite paring knife. We had several hills of pumpkins in the garden because we canned pumpkin for making pumpkin pies. Pumpkin pie was a staple on the Sunday dinner table for the winter months, especially if it was our turn to feed the circuit preacher after church. Uncle Clyde said he wasn't sure what was taught in seminaries, except eating. Every preacher that ate at our table ate like a horse.

I also loved Halloween because we made our own costumes, and Uncle Clyde drove us into town so we could trick or treat. Our costumes were never of some cartoon character made by some child labor factory in China. Our costumes were a product of what we had and our imagination. I dressed as a pirate once. Uncle Clyde cut me a patch for one eye out of an old car tire inner tube. I carried a real sword which my grandfather brought home from France in WWI. I wore a white shirt, black pants, one of grandmother's scarves around my head for a bandana. I looked pretty good and unlike today's ready make masks, I could actually see (out of one eye). Uncle Clyde told me when I was older that one elderly lady who gave me a homemade popcorn ball for a treat, said "So you're a pirate?" "Yes mama." I said. "Where are your buccaneers?" "I don't know mama." was my reply. Uncle Clyde said I should have told her they were under my bandana. My brothers and I took turns being ghosts, witches, cowboys, and Indians, and we never spent a penny on a costume. The kids today that come by my house for trick or treat all have expensive costumes. They are not as scary as their tattooed and body pierced parents standing at the top of my driveway chain smoking cigarettes and talking about what was on the Jerry Springer show that day.

We seldom received store bought candy as treats. Apples, pears, homemade fudge or peanut brittle were the most common treats. The treats we give out today are too much. I understand people are afraid to receive home baked goods today, because some newscaster reported that a kid got a brownie with a razor blade in it while trick or treating at a crack house in east L.A. I have also heard parents tell their kids to avoid any homemade chocolates, because they may have Ex-lax in them. I have taken Ex-lax. Any kid can tell the difference between Ex-lax and chocolate. Chocolate is sweet and has that wonderful cocoa fragrance, Ex-lax stinks and it taste like what it makes you do. Some of Mrs. Richardson's home made peanut brittle was sharp enough to cut your tongue if you were not careful and Mrs. Martin's yellow apples were still green and would give me the runs.

No, today we give little bite size pieces of name brand candy bars that are advertised every 5 minutes during Saturday morning children's TV shows. They may have been considered penny candy once, but at today's prices each piece is more like 25 cents. What's more, kids today feel insulted if they are given just one piece of candy. They have been taught by their parents to just keep holding the bag out until the home owner tosses in a handful, or better yet, hands the kid the candy dish. I know we spent 40 bucks on trick or treat candy last year. We bought it in September. The candy sits in our cupboard tempting me for 2 months every time I reach in to get a handful of Fiber Therapy capsules. My wife also keeps inventory of the candy weekly. If she sees a bag of miniature M&M's opened, as I walk through the door after a hard day at the store, she hits me. "Did you know there are only 47 little bags of candy in this package of 48?"

I can't sneak one little candy bar. No, we have to save the candy for the little goblins so they can keep a week long sugar high and bounce off the walls at school, just after the teachers had recovered from the kid's hyper fix caused by cotton candy and elephant ears eaten at the County Fair.

GUNS

A hot topic today is the 2nd Amendment of The Constitution. This amendment covers the right to keep and bear arms. Ohio has joined other states in passing a concealed carry law.

Health care is becoming less and less affordable for the average working family. The national debt has gone through the ceiling again. We still travel a two lane cow path (highway) when traveling west out of our county. All these things are not being discussed by our legislators. But, By God we can carry a Smith and Wesson 357 Magnum Revolver. I guess they are just playing to the home crowd.

I am concerned about six pack Charlie carrying a 9mm Ruger in the glove compartment of his pick-up truck. What if he comes into my store mad about his water heater not working and he decides to get his pistol and shoot a hole in our display water heater. I know some of my customers. If their shooting ability is anything like their home repair skills; they won't be able to hit the broad side of a barn, they would miss and really do me harm by hitting my computer.

Anyway, guns have played a role in most of my families' traditions. I have used shotguns and rifles since I was a little fellow. My tour of duty in the Army taught me how to use grenade launchers, mortars, howitzers, and the grand daddy of them all, the 50 caliber machine gun. I think I could still field strip an M16 blindfolded and I could probably change a red hot barrel on a machine gun and re-gap the firing pin using the "go-no go gauge". So guns are important to me. In fact I probably would not be married today, if it weren't for guns.

My father in-law Edmund, a young handsome coal miner met and fell in love with a young maiden by the name of Rose. It was during the Great Depression and Edmund and his buddy in the coal mine worked extra hard to earn money for a nice wedding. At three cents a ton for digging coal, you really had to be in love to work extra and save twenty dollars for a wedding. After exchanging their vows in St. John Vianny Church in Belmont County, the wedding party and guest adjourned to the room over the United Mineworkers Union Hall. Edmond had twelve siblings and Rose came from a family of thirteen; add in cousins, aunts, and uncles, plus parish members and guys on his coal mine shift, the Union Hall was packed.

After cutting the cake and throwing the bride's garter, the night settled into the real purpose, dancing and drinking. The orchestra consisted of a squeeze box (accordion), clarinet and a piano player. The group's repertoire consisted of one jitter bug and lots of polkas. Although Prohibition was in effect, the best man was selling shots of Canadian Whiskey and a dance with the bride for one dollar. When the Canadian Whiskey ran out, several brothers had B.O.J. (brought their own jug). It seems abandoned coal mine entrances made excellent places to hide a still from the Revenuers. This money would be used to buy furniture from the coal company store to furnish the little house they were to rent in the coal company's housing camp.

As the night wore on, Edmond's brother Pete got a little too much hooch in his snoot. Pete got into an argument with brother Mike, and the next thing everyone knew, brother Check pulled out a gun to try and break up the fight. A scuffle ensued, and the gun discharged, shooting out the double hung window facing the street. Chaos broke out with most folks heading for the stairs. Pete sobered up a little and said, "Wow, is this what they call a shot gun wedding?

WHAT MALL IS THAT NEAR?

—◻—

I have friends who changed careers and moved to a new position in Minnesota. In an effort to entice us to visit, they offered their home as a "base of operation", as we would have said in the Army. Instead of attacking an enemy during Army maneuver training, their base of operation would be used to attack Minnesota's new tourist site, The Mall of America.

The Mall of America is to shoppers as Mecca is to faithful Muslims, Cooperstown is to baseball fans or Talladega is to NASCAR enthusiasts. My wife and daughter took up our friends' offer and made not one, but three pilgrimages to the Mall of America.

This mammoth shrine erected for compulsory shoppers from all over the world sits on hundreds of acres of what were once prime soy bean fields (I bet Minnesota didn't have a good land use plan in effect). Instead of the land being used to feed the world, the land is now helping feed our country's national per capita credit card debt. Instead of growing millions of bushels of the nutritious peas, the land has 1,040 men and women's bathrooms where millions of shoppers take a pee.

The land that once had fence rows that provided a refuge for quail and pheasants, this land now has stores with names like Thomas Kinkade Galleries, Perfume-Mania, Bow Wow, and Lake Woebegone where some "strange birds" hang out.

The land that once had a beautiful winter landscape with snow drifts is now overrun by teenage girls showing their midriffs. The land that was once a feeding stop for migrating geese is now home to over 86 restaurants and fast food shops dispensing all sorts of artery clogging sweet or greasy processed foods.

Growing up on the farm, most of our food needs we raised or we grew ourselves. Basic staples like nails, twine, tools, or light bulbs could be purchased or traded at Pascal General Store down the lane from the farm house. For other needs like bolts of fabric, pots and pans, spices and bicycle parts, we dressed up and went into town on Saturday morning. So did our neighbors. Church and the Court House steps were gathering places for folks who worked the land all week. If you couldn't find it on Main Street, chances are we didn't need it or couldn't afford it anyway. For those really special items all we needed to do was look thru the Sears and Roebuck, Montgomery Ward, Western Auto, or Burpee Seed Catalogs and order.

We didn't have yard sales back home either. Yard sales today are full of things we had to have, that ended up under foot, then in the garage, until we need to make more storage room, so we can buy more things we don't need.

This addiction to Mall shopping has reached an epidemic status among young people, male and female. To prove my point, I asked my daughter who lives in Columbus, an intelligent, college educated modern woman, to pick-up for me a special toilet flush valve at a wholesale plumbing supply business on Morse Road. I gave her directions over the phone and based on the pause in our conversation, I thought she was just writing down my instructions. The pause was caused by her not recognizing exactly where Morse Road is in Columbus. Then she asked the question I was afraid she would ask, "What Mall is that near, Easton or Polaris?"

Where did I go wrong as a parent? How did we spoil our youth with all this modern material stuff? Life is just too fast paced today, too many choices, too technical.

Well got to go, I just saw the UPS truck stop out front. Maybe he has my new Italian Bicycle racing shoes I bought on E-bay. I sent the seller a digital picture of my bike's pedals and he said they will fit. I have already wired the money to Rome. Do as I say, I've often told my daughter....

MORE HOME REMEDIES

—⊡—

A friend of mine asked to speak to me in private the other day. I always think the worst when someone calls me aside to talk. Maybe they have an illness, their spouse left them or worse yet, they backed their truck over my new bicycle. With modern medicine, illness can be cured, you can always find another spouse, but to have to find and break in a new bike, well, that could be a crisis.

"I have hemorrhoids." David said. I knew he could be a pain in that region figuratively, but now he has that problem literally. We have shared lots of personal feelings and emotions down through the years but my question was, "Why are you telling me?" He said he reads my columns in the Tribune, and remembers reading about my grandmother's home remedy that cured my father's derriere. In that column I described grandmother mixing up a batch of pickling alum and ice cold water in a pickle crock, in which my father soaked away his swollen tissue. I went on to say that we sold that old pickling crock to some organic yuppie bent on preservative free food processing. That's why I don't eat pickles that say organic on the label.

"Why don't you just see your family physician?" I asked. "I play golf with my doctor; I can't let him know that I have, you know, that I have those things." David said.

I asked David if he wanted me to whip up a batch of ice cold alum water soak for him. "Not yet," he said. "Find out what your friends and family that live out of town are doing, and keep it quiet." Why did he not want anyone to know he had hemorrhoids and why did he think all my friends and family had hemorrhoids?

So I began asking. First I asked my cousin, whose family has always been a pain. She said one of her relatives uses a popular over the counter ointment in a tube. She also said this relative rubbed this hemorrhoid ointment under her baggy eyes to tighten the skin and make her look younger.

I called my brother-in-law Wade, who lives in California. Californians think everything they do is better in the Golden State. He is kind of an organic, holistic, left coast guy. Wade said he should buy California avocados, cut them up, put in a blender, combine with an Aloe plant and make a paste. Refrigerate and apply as needed.

David is a big boned fellow (large), so I thought I would call my Army buddy in Texas, since everything is big in Texas. Bernie didn't have a good thing to say about anything unless it was done in the Lone Star State. Biggest state fair, biggest ranches, biggest BBQ's, biggest steaks...and so on. Our company commander (Capt. Rush) was from Oklahoma. To put Bernie in his place, from time to time Capt. Rush would remind Bernie that if it wasn't for Oklahoma Cowboys and Mexican Senoritas, there would not be any Texans. Bernie said he would ship us a Saguaro Cactus Plant. We should cut the Cactus and bleed the liquid (cactus juice). Soak gauze in the cactus juice, refrigerate, and apply as a compress. Left over juice can also be used to treat poison ivy and sunburn.

Dave tried all four remedies. For him the Saguaro Cactus remedy worked best. Being the entrepreneur, he is thinking of packaging and marketing the avocado and cactus products for QVC. He has contacted the lady on QVC that pitches Diamonique Toe Ring Jewelry on their late night show, when only insomniacs (who can't sleep because, among other things, they have piles) are watching. They sell everything else on TV, beauty products, secret weight loss pills, cookware, and clothing: why not sell some home remedies? Maybe David could get fixed financially as well as physically.

BIRDS AND BEES AND PIGS

—▣—

When my daughter was younger she was very inquisitive. I remember watching a movie with her when she was five years old. The movie was "Old Yeller". We both cried at the end (I still cry when I see that movie), but the part I remember most was Old Yeller's mate giving birth to litter of puppies. My daughter asked the question, "Where do puppies come from?" I knew this birds and bees question would come up sooner or later, so I had rehearsed some lines. Before I could begin she asked, "Where do babies come from?"

I began to get nervous, there were butterflies in my stomach, but I took a deep breath and began. "You came out of your mother's belly." Before I could get out any more of my prepared words, my daughter asked "How did I get in my mothers belly?" That question threw me off course. I hastily responded with "Daddy planted a seed." "How did you get your seed in mommy's belly?" she asked. I was now frazzled by this curious five year old child. Without thinking I said, "Daddy rubbed his body against mommy's body to get a seed inside." By now my wife was on the floor rolling in laughter. Sweat was rolling down my forehead and my face was beet red. I was thinking to my self, 'Why can't she learn the facts of life like I did?" I learned from Uncle Clyde, observing the action in the barn yard and eventually in the hay loft.

When I was growing up on the farm, I saw first hand

what the birds and bees were all about. The procreation constantly going on in the barn yard taught me about male and female anatomy, mating rituals, courtships and copulation. Breeding was an economic fact of life on the farm, the more baby chicks, calves and pigs that were born, the more money the farm made. The more money we had for store bought stuff.

There was more action and noise in the pasture when our bull was courting a young heifer than any "B" movie I saw in my Alpha Gamma Rho Fraternity house in college. The roosters were the most aggressive of all the farm animals. Roosters took great pride in inflicting pain on their subject hen, and of course they had to brag (crow) about their feat. I think the pigs enjoyed reproducing the most. The boar and the sow took their time to develop the moment by not hurrying the foreplay. Their jowls became flush (pink) afterwards and they always took a nap.

Uncle Clyde said the pigs were the smartest animals on our farm. I agree, they enjoyed eating, sleeping playing, they just enjoyed life. There was probably a life lesson there, whether I saw it or not.

Uncle Clyde also enjoyed life, sometimes too much for my Grandmother's liking. Uncle Clyde courted the ladies more than any bull, rooster or boar we had on the farm. I think Grandmother was more interested in Uncle Clyde's chores than his libido, and threatened to put saltpeter in his mashed potatoes. I asked Uncle Clyde what was salt peter, and what does it do. He explained the Army put it in the soldier's food on troop ships to stifle sexual desire. He said its effects wore off as soon as they made port in Italy and were greeted by the local young Italian signoras. When I was in Army boot camp the Mess Sergeant said he put salt peter in our scrambled eggs. I was like Uncle Clyde, as soon as I earned the first week end pass; the effects wore off as soon as I made it through the gates of the military base. Perhaps the farm lessons just weren't learned well enough. Perhaps Uncle Clyde's lessons were.

WHERE IS THE BEST PLACE TO EAT?

—▫—

I appreciate all the comments from Tribune readers about little anecdotes I have written about this past year or so. Most of my writings have been about growing up on a small farm or my tour of duty in the Army. Lots of readers have contributed their own spin on my experiences. It just goes to show you what a small world we really live in. Readers have shared with me almost exact experiences on farms in Ohio, Maine, Florida, Washington, Alabama, and Texas. Veterans of all our Wars and all branches of services have shared with me similar experiences of military life, be it in 1944 in the South Pacific, 1953 in Korea, 1968 in Vietnam, or 1970's in Europe.

Some readers have suggested I write about a common theme of any soldier, sailor, or airman, the search for local entertainment. For those that remember travel before the interstates, a common practice was to pull into a gas station and ask for a good place to eat and what to see locally. This same method is used by G.I.'s when sailing into a new port, landing at a new air base, or being stationed at a new post, only our question was, "Where is the off limits red light district?

Red Light Districts in most countries and in many cultures act as a community center for homesick travelers. After all, prostitution is the world's oldest profession. Keep in mind the following is based as volunteered information from Tribune readers and are not necessarily the personal experiences of this writer.

Ft. Campbell, KY is home of the 101st U.S. Army Airborne Division. Pauline's in Bowling Green KY has been as much a ritual in parachute training as spit shining your first pair of Jump boots and getting wings tattooed on your left arm. Pauline's Stable was well stocked by young professionals. These ladies would come to Pauline's and perform what they felt was a patriotic tour of duty.

Prostitution is legal and taxed in much of Europe. Drei Farbe Haus (House of Three Colors) was in Stuttgart, Germany. This three story building is directly across from the City Hall, which adds an air of authority to the three madams (one for each level). The lower level contains the best looking, most expensive ladies, the third level the cheapest. It is said upon entering there is a sign that reads in four languages, "soldiers and sailors use elevator to third floor". The third floor stable of ladies consists of all shapes, sizes, colors, and national origins.

Subic Bay, Philippines has a street area named Olongo City. An area about two miles long, in which there are strip clubs, tattoo parlors and sporting houses. Most sailors wait until they are stateside to get their tattoos because of the uncleanness of the Philippines. Ironically, they don't hesitate to mate with the ladies of the night.

Qui Nhon, Vietnam, had Madame Ngu's Pleasure Palace. The menu was in dollars, MPC (military pay certificates), c-rations, cigarettes or chocolate bars. Mama San took the money and the girls all wanted to marry a G.I. and live in America.

In Naples, Italy, the economy revolves around small family owned businesses. Whore houses are no exception and many line the road leading to the U.S. Navy Port. Domani's was a small family bar that served meals. The father was the bartender, the mother the cook and the daughters, well, it is a family business. Many times, I am told, sailors would drop in, down several beers and lots of pasta, only to be told "Domani" (Domani means tomorrow in Italian). It seems these daughters were more of a tease than actual bill of fare.

I have many more similar stories from fellow veterans to share with Tribune readers. Maybe we can publish them in a Travel Guide and insert into a Sunday Tribune. Perhaps it could be called a Tricktik.

BEAUJOLAIS NOUVEAU

—◻—

At exactly one minute past midnight on the third Thursday of each November, sixty five million bottles of French Beaujolais Nouveau wine begin their journey to snobs on all seven continents. "Le Beaujolais Nouveau est arrive!" banners proclaim this frivolous ritual throughout the "civilized world". The precious jugs (not bottles) of this cheap red wine is delivered by jets to New York and other habitats of the rich and famous. What's more, instead of sniffing the cork, swirling the crystal goblet and chewing the wine, Beaujolais Nouveau is enjoyed by gulping, rather than sipping.

I had the honor of uncorking a jug of Beaujolais Nouveau myself when I was in the Army stationed in Europe. It was such a festive event. Somewhat like a chug-a-lug contest at a fraternity party. I was in the company of a German medical student, an Iranian business man, a Swiss school teacher and a French carpenter and they all acted the same, drunk and stupid. These were folks who lived in my apartment building and we enjoyed each others companionship at several dinner parties previously. At those parties, wines' pedigrees were studied and experienced. Sherbet and sorbet were used to cleanse the pallet between bottles. The Beaujolais Nouveau party was more like being at a hay wagon red neck party back home.

My father was a great wine maker. My father's wine

was not made from the Camay, Pinet noir, Charardonnay, Merlot, or Zinfandel grapes. His wine was made from wild purple grapes. I helped pick them on the hillside by the springhouse. Father also made wine from mulberries, black berries, rhubarb, and dandelions. After we picked the grapes we took them to Uncle Clyde, who ran them through his cider press. I always wanted to smash the grapes with my feet the way Uncle Clyde said they did in Italy, when he was there during WWII. Uncle Clyde wouldn't let me because he said my toe jam would get in the juice and ruin the wine. We took the squeezing from the press and filtered them through cheese cloth into a big crock. My father added sugar until he obtained the secret sweetness he was looking for. After the juice settled a few days we funneled it into an old charred oak barrel that was once used to age Heaven Hill Bourbon. Once full, the barrel was corked and a rubber tube inserted into a hole in the cork. Paraffin was poured around the hole and the other end of the tube was looped to the floor of the spring house and inserted into a bucket of water. As the wine fermented, the gases would boil off into the water, but no air got into the barrel. My father warned me that if I tried to sample the wine before it was time; air would get in and turn the whole lot into vinegar. When no more bubbles could be seen in the water jug, it was time to tap the barrel and put the wine in gallon jugs. Uncle Clyde would then invite neighbors and friends that first Saturday night after bottling the wine. They all met in the barn lean to, smoked cigars and drank the wine out of coffee cups.

My grandmother didn't approve of such drinking,

but my father quoted the Bible's 1st Timothy 5:23 in an attempt to justify hitting the juice. That's the bible passage that Paul tells Timothy to "Drink no longer just water, but use a little wine for the stomach's sake and thine often infirmities." My father could always seem to find a bible passage condoning whatever it was he was doing that his mother didn't approve of. My experience with Beaujolais Nouveau was about the same as my father's experience with his new wild grape home made wine. A big cheap red wine hangover.

Too Much Trash

—◻—

I took a day off from work here awhile back and the first thing my wife asked me to do was, take out the trash.

I hauled two heavy plastic trash cans to the curb. I looked down the street and every house had two cans. My neighborhood is mainly empty nesters. Our kids are grown or off to college. Why with only two per household do we all have two cans?

When I was a kid growing up on our family farm, we didn't have any trash cans. We were taught to clean our dinner plates, so the few table scraps were fed to our dog, Blackie, or to the chickens. Chickens will eat anything.

Since we grew our own vegetables, and canned in mason jars, butchered and smoked our own meat, had our own orchard, fished and hunted, we did not have any packaging trash. What few things we bought from the grocery store, such as flour, corn meal, and sugar were packed in cloth bags which were recycled into kitchen aprons or shop rags. We bought a few things in metal cans like coffee. The coffee cans were recycled into containers to store bolts and nails. Now and again we would order something from the Sears or Montgomery Ward catalog and we would have a cardboard box, but that too became a storage container or needles and thread. When Grandmother bought her first electric range for the kitchen, that big cardboard box made a perfect fort for my brothers and me. We bought Kendall motor oil in glass jars. After an oil change, the jars were cleaned and used to put up pickles and the old motor oil was spread on our lane to keep the dust down.

My Uncle Clyde developed a taste for Heinz Tomato Ketchup while he was in the Army and my father took a liking to Old Spice when he was in the Marines. The bottles were used for target practice with my 22 caliber bolt action single shot rifle.

So how did I go from no trash in an extended family of 9 people on a farm to 2 large plastic trash cans every week with just me and my city slicker wife?

I decided to inventory my trash and see why. Pizza boxes, Lean Cuisine and Slim Fast boxes and cans take up a lot of space in our trash and seem to not do what we bought them for (to lose weight). Junk mail, Ice Cream boxes, pop cans, margarine tubs, salsa jars, under arm deodorant cans, etc., etc., etc. We never had all this stuff when I was a kid on the farm. Even if times have changed, do we need to throw all this away? Isn't there a way to recycle all this trash? If so how would we do it?

I had an idea when I was riding my bicycle the other day. I rode by a man who had a big black plastic sack on his back. He was hauling pop cans to the scrap yard were they are crushed and shipped to China. It must be hard work, because I saw him later that day and it appeared he had worked so hard that he sweated through his clothing, including his pants! He was trying to re-hydrate himself with some kind of liquid in a bottle covered with a brown paper sack.

Now if we had lots of folks like him that could come around and pick-up our paper, glass, and metal cans and take them to the recycle stations, we would not have to use precious farm land for garbage dumps. We could use that farm land to build big new super stores. Then every ten years abandon the big ugly building and let the weeds grow in the parking lot. The big new super stores would be stocked with Chinese manufactured goods and fattening processed foods, giving us more cardboard, paper, metal, and glass to export to third world countries for recycling.

Life was sure simpler when I had chickens.

RIGID CALENDAR

—▫—

We're at the point in the year when it seems everyone resolves to change something for the New Year. Lots of folks resolve to lose weight in the New Year. Exercising more is probably another resolution people make for the up coming months too. Spending more time with loved ones is another item folks resolve to do. My experience has been less than a success on my own past new year's resolutions, but it does give me time to reminisce.

Growing up on the farm, New Years was not much of a holiday, and Grandmother didn't need to resolve anything anyway. She just looked to the Good Book, and moved on from there. I think she always hoped Uncle Clyde would pick up on the concept and move away from the crooked path towards the straight and narrow. Uncle Clyde preferred the windy, more colorful path.

The New Year holiday just passed without much notice on the farm. The eggs still needed gathered, the cows still needed milked, firewood needed gathered and kindling split. Actually, there wasn't much time for reflection and by the time midnight rolled around and the new year started, if you weren't asleep, you were probably on the Uncle Clyde path.

The change in the year did mean a change in the calendars hung around the farm house, barn, and out buildings. Grandmother's calendar in the kitchen was from Wayne Feeds. It had a bucolic rural scene that was supposed to remind us that farmers were the backbone of civilization throughout mankind. There were scenes of shepards in the fields tending their flock as well as cows in the pasture and a little boy with a red bandana and a cane pole headed for his favorite fishing hole. The feed calendars were easy to obtain from the feed mill down the lane. Uncle Clyde and Grandfather kept the Burley Tobacco Seed calendars out in the barns. Those Burley Tobacco Seed calendars gave me a hint of the female form. They were harder to come by, as you had to ask for them from the seed salesman and they came in a brown paper sleeve so wondering eyes would not see Miss January sitting on the sack of seed in a halter top. By today's standards, the calendars were pretty tame, but certainly they were risqué' enough for banishment from the house.

Bobby Ray's father worked in a factory. A tool salesmen from Elyria, Ohio that called on his shop gave him the best calendar of all. The Ridge Tool Calendar he brought home in his lunch bucket was the talk of the lane. The young ladies who posed with pipe wrenches and tubing benders would cause any young man's heart to beat faster. Some of my favorite dreams were about being on a beach with Miss May and her holding a pipe reamer. Bobby Ray had a crush on Miss August who posed in a two piece swimsuit next to a K-380 Drain Auger. We kept the Rigid Tool Calendar in the Smoke House, and made sure a ham was hanging in front so Grandmother couldn't see. Grandfather would gaze through the months saying he was looking for the pipe dies. He wasn't fooling me. Uncle Clyde used to quip "Keep a Rigid Tool" when giving his farewell to a friend

(I guess if he were alive today he would say, see your doctor about Viagra). The Rigid Tool Calendar satisfied the two most powerful male instincts, pretty women and good tools. I would like to thank my friend Dave with helping me reminisce about calendars. Dave grew up in Coshocton, the birthplace of advertising calendars. Dave remembers the Rigid Tool Calendars also. Dave is really good when it comes to residential electrical systems. Dave said he was just looking at the months with Rigid Electrical Pliers, keeping abreast (nod, nod, wink, wink) of new developments. He's not fooling me any more than Grandfather.

FURNITURE

My wife wanted a piece of furniture for Christmas. She likes that country furnishing look in our home. She is a city girl and why she wants our house to look like "Little House on the Prairie" is beyond me. But, being a good husband, I gave her a gift of money for Christmas, so she could buy the country sideboard she wanted.

She bought it and brought it home. I kept quiet, for a while. Then, I just couldn't take it any more. I am a very sensitive guy and I did not want to hurt her feelings, but I tried to explain to her that her sideboard was made out of cheap number two pine. It was assembled with drywall screws (not even recessed and filled with wood putty). In fact the damn thing almost fell apart while I was trying to maneuver it into the spot she had cleared in the family room. The wood had been beaten with chains to give the impression that time had produced the little dents. The finish looked like the maker started with one color, ran out of that, and went to another can of paint to finish. The whole piece looked cheap. If I had made something like that in seventh grade wood shop class, I would have received the grade of D (poor). Edges were not sanded smooth. Hinges were not mortised. I had to use wedges to get the thing to sit level on the floor.

"But", she says defensively, "it is the style, that down home country look." We never had furniture like that in our farmhouse. What little furniture we had in our farmhouse was made by craftsmen, with pride. Our furniture was practical, like the pie safe in the Parlor. It was rubbed and sanded, finished with shellac and the drawers were dovetailed. The Hoosier cupboard in the kitchen was very useful with compartments for flour, a sifter, a rolling pin, a cutting board, and well fitting doors. Our four post feather beds were solid, sturdy and had plenty of room for storage and a "thunder mug" underneath.

As I look around my home with all this "country furniture", I wonder how others will view my furnishings, say 100 years from now. When my grandparents bought the family farm in 1900 they sparsely furnished the rooms, but what they did have was quality. One hundred years later, when we sold the farm, its equipment and its furnishings, the furniture by then was considered antique, and brought good money.

I proposed this scenario to my wife as a way of having her look at the style of furnishings in the text of lasting aesthetics and value. I made up a story. "In the year 2004 a dormant volcano under Spring Mountain (Mount Saint Spring Mountain) erupted and buried our neighborhood under a hundred feet of volcanic ash. The area was abandoned until the year 2104, when President George W.W.W.W. Bush III, sent an expedition to the area to excavate the ruins and try to understand the culture that had been buried alive. As the archeologist worked their way up our street, they uncovered my neighbor's house with his contemporary furnishings, and collection of military paraphernalia. The archeologist would determine this was a middle class family's dwelling with a small museum. The archeologist would move onto another neighbor's and uncover his boat, jet skis, and motor cycle. An anthropologist would deduct this was a hip family with lots of disposable income. Then the excavators would unearth my home. 'Oh my', Mr. Jones (Indiana Jones) would say, 'Look at their furniture. Look how poor the materials and craftsmanship are. This must be where the poor people lived." "Get it?" I asked my wife. "We should furnish our house as if it were in Pompeii and would be studied by anthropologists in the future," I said. "Pompeii" she said, "What does our house have to do with Italian food?"

Go Cut Me a Switch

I read a startling statistic in the newspaper the other day. The article stated that 21% of kids ages 9 to 17 have a diagnosable mental addictive disorder. Attention-deficit hyperactivity disorder was the most diagnosed and deals with youngsters having problems following directions and staying on a task in school.

Wow! Most of my family and all of my friends were afflicted with the same behavior, only we called it being ornery or spunky.

As I read on, it became apparent why so many of our kids are labeled with a condition that requires medication to regulate. "Many advocates worry that mental-health disorders are over-diagnosed and youths aren't given options such as counseling. Nearly 40,000 Ohio children on Medicaid were taking behavior drugs at a cost of $65.5 million." It's all about money; lots of folks are making money on these kids. Instead of drugs, how about a good old fashioned butt whipping?

I received a good many whippings as a kid, all deserved I'm sure. With 5 kids in our family, it seems my father was either telling one of us to go cut our own switch off a tree in the orchard, taking off his belt or getting the big wooden spoon out of the kitchen. Discipline was a family tradition, passed from generation to generation.

My Grandfather was born in 1875 and farmed all his life. His hands were hard and his knuckles huge. I asked Grandfather once why he had such big hands. He told me he went to a one room school house and a major part of learning back then was to get up in front of the class and recite your lesson. That always made Grandfather nervous, and he would chew on his wooden pencil when nervous. The school master would take a heavy wooden ruler and smack the kid's knuckles if they talked in class or chewed their pencil. No Ritalin for my Grandfather, just the wooden ruler.

My Grandmother told me that my father acted up in school now and then too. In fact my father was expelled from school once. My father and Uncle Clyde bought some M80 cherry bombs and took them to school. The one room school houses were gone by then and they went to a consolidated school, complete with indoor plumbing. Uncle Clyde had thrown a cherry bomb in mean Miss Olive's outhouse and thought that was funny, but when he and my father threw a cherry bomb in the porcelain toilets at school, it wasn't funny. The explosion flooded the first floor of the school. No Prozac to change their mood, but a one week expulsion from school, a shaving leather strap whipping at home and a week's extra hard labor on the farm, plus they had to buy the school a new toilet.

I was not a perfect child growing up either. My Father always quoted the Bible passage that said "spare the rod, spoil the child." When ever we traveled in the family car, mainly to Church, one of us 5 kids in the back seat had to goose someone. The resulting sibling squabble ended with a stern "Don't make me stop this car" or a swift backhand to the bobbing head of me or one of my ornery brothers. In high school, instead of a prescription of Zoloft, I got three licks with a huge wooden paddle by the Principal for peeling out (leaving rubber) in the student parking lot with my 1956 Chevy.

In the Army we had an unauthorized form of discipline to make troops pay attention to detail, the Blanket Party. The squad leader would throw a heavy olive drab wool blanket over the un-cooperative soldier, and the rest of the squad would whip him into shape by a few whacks with their rifle butts. This was a very effective lesson.

Maybe the State of Ohio needs to allow more corporal and less medical fixes for behavior.

FUTURE CANDIDATES
QUALIFICATION TEST

—🔲—

This year's political campaign has really drained my brain. I feel dizzy after watching debates and political ads on TV. My eyes glaze over after reading editorials in the newspapers or all the direct mail pieces each candidate sends me. I have whiplash after driving to work every day looking at all the campaign yard signs. There must be a better way to find out how a candidate stands on issues.

Now that I think about it, we should borrow a page for the Army Recruiters. When entering the U.S. Army we were required to take the ASVAB, Armed Forces Vocational Aptitude Battery. Here are some sample questions: A magnet will attract: A. water B. a flower C. a cloth rag D. a nail. If twelve workers are needed to run 4 machines, how many workers are needed to run 20? A. 20 B. 48 C. 60 D. 80.

The results from this test help the Army determine whether you are qualified to be a Cannon Cocker (carry artillery shells), a Grunt (carry a rifle), or a Tread Head (drive a main battle tank). If you were really smart and did well on the test you could get a gravy job where you didn't have to do much, like aide de camp (Generals gopher) or Battalion Liaison (no one knows what this job entails, similar to a consultant in the business world today). If you did poorly on the test, then you were recommended for Infantry Officer Candidate School. By the way, I was an Infantry Officer.

I would name this test the C.C.S.T. (Candidates Common Sense Test). The test would be designed to explore the innermost thoughts of those running for political office and would be administered in a clinical setting after sodium pentothal (truth serum) is given. Here are some sample questions:

1. If on a fishing trip you forget to bring the bottle opener, which of the following would you use to open your beer: A. Belt buckle B. Fishing pliers C. Boat Anchor D. Teeth

2. Define a Junket: A. What you should do with accumulated stuff in your garage B. A small wooden boat C. An exotic vacation taken at tax payer's expense and disguised as a fact finding trip. D. A piece of a necklace containing your former intern's picture.

3. When faced with a recession and limited funds you would: A. Cut Medicare payments B. Cut education spending C. Give yourself a pay raise D. All of the above.

4. Duties of an intern include: A. Making coffee B. Typing C. Using cigars D. Ordering pizza

5. Contributions to political campaigns are used to: A. Inform the voters of the issues B. Give jobs to my in-laws C. Fund rallies to boost my own ego D. Allow for intelligent debates.

6. A deficit is: A. Spending money you do not have. B. What you pick up when walking your dog C. What Republicans cause D. What Democrats cause.

7. Kickbacks are: A. What a chainsaw does when in a bind B. What a mule does C. Illegal money received from

Government Contractors D. All of the above.

8. An ethics committee: A. Investigates wrong doing B. Nurses who administer a gas before an operation C. Is used to hoodwink the public D. A smoke screen.

9. Constituents are: A. The people you serve B. What laxatives are use to relief C. People from Conneaut, Ohio D. Gullible people

10. Most of the money collected for Political campaigns are used: A. for TV Ads B. for Radio Ads C. Travel expenses D. Siphoned off into my retirement fund.

Did you take the Test? How did you do? The correct answers are as follows:

    1 – D
    2 – A
    3 – D
    4 – C
    5 – B or C
    6 – C and D
    7 – D
    8 – C and D
    9 – D
   10 – D

PARENTS, PLEASE TEACH
YOUR CHILDREN WELL

—▫—

The other day I was helping carry out a customers paint purchase. As I was putting the paint cans in the lady's trunk, I noticed a shinny penny laying in the parking lot. Without hesitation I bent over, picked up the penny and said a phrase I heard my father say a thousand times. "See a penny, pick it up and all the day you will have good luck". Well the kid wrangler and her five year old boy were dumbfounded by my actions. "What did he say", the little boy asked. "Something about picking up junk in the parking lot", the mother explained as she was seat belting her young'en.

We as elders have a responsibility to dispense wisdom to the youth and the best way is repeating corny phrases, allegories or like Jesus, parables. I heard Mathew Chapter 13 thousands of times. I remember Jesus teaching, "As you sow, so shall you reap".

Mark Twain used little allegories to poke humor at real life observations and teach lessons too. Take his quote "whiskey is for drinking; water is for fighting over". He was teaching us about how precious good water is to a farmer.

Will Rogers also used corny phrases to teach us about things that are important. I use one of his phrases to teach my employees that we can all be good at something. Wil said, "Everybody is ignorant, only on different subjects".

"Don't make me stop this car" was my father's most used phrase. He warned me that if my brothers and I did not stop poking each other in the back seat of our 1954 Chevy Coupe, he was going to pull over to the side of the road and give us a good belt whipping.

"Straighten up or I will tan you hide", was another favorite of my father's. Again used mostly to stop sibling fighting.

"I brought you into this world, I can take you out of this world too", was my fathers way of saying to me and my brothers to sit up straight and stop giggling in church.

"Early to bed, early to rise is the way to be happy, healthy, and wise", was his way of telling us to turn off the radio and go to sleep.

My grandfather used phrases also. Whenever I helped him repair a fence or build a new outhouse, he would always say, "measure twice, cut once". I wish I could instill that phrase in the sub-conscience of some of my customers today. If they could think "measure twice, cut once" they would not be bringing back products they claim are "defective" when in fact they didn't read the directions and screwed it up.

My mother only used one corny phrase, "wait until your father gets home". I normally took her advice and stopped aggravating her, knowing my father would get the belt after me.

Sergeant Ricker, my drill instructor in boot camp

used phrases too in his quest to mold my platoon into "a lean mean fighting machine" as he would say. "Stay alert, stay alive" was used a zillion times during training to make us realize we need to pay attention or we could be killed. "One grenade will get you all" is another Sergeant Ricker would use when we would bunch up (get too close) in a force march. Sergeant Ricker also used phrases to teach us how to behave when we got leave and went off base in our "civvies" (civilian clothing). One of the bits of wisdom Sergeant Ricker embedded in my mind is still with me every day. As we waited for the bus to take us to the "real world" just outside the gate at Ft. Benning, He would say "Men, you should only be afraid of two things...women and the police".

WATCH THE WEATHER CHANNEL

—◻—

I take the basic cable TV subscription. It is great to have 70 channels to flick through during the evening. It is a powerful feeling to be able to push a button to bypass Katie Couric if I feel her newscast is too "perky". Likewise if Fox News' Ann Coulter is pontificating on a hard right wing view of the world, I can flick right past her. I seem to always end up on the History or Discovery channels anyway. It's just that power the remote gives me to show those media moguls who is the boss.

When I was growing up, we only had three channels of TV reception and the duty to use the rotary knob that changed the channels was given to the youngest child. I was the oldest sibling and when I began to have homework and other nightly chores on the farm; my parents bore another child, so my father would have someone to change the TV channel. Maybe that's what we need to give all the poor people in third world countries to control their exploding populations, TV's and remotes. The men in these developing nations, would flick through all the channels, fall asleep in their easy chair and hence not conceive another child. Birth control without hormones or sterilization.

Back to my current 70 TV channels. Every channel seems flooded with negative political commercials. These commercials are a parade of unflattering pictures and finger pointing about raising taxes and loss of jobs.

Being a politician myself for the last 10 months, I have seen some interesting people in elected offices. Why is it when an elected official gets caught with his hand in the cookie jar, he checks into an alcohol rehabilitation facility and/or he finds religion?

It is a tribute to our form of government that despite the drunks, liars, cheats, adulterers and pedophiles we have in some elected offices, bridges get built, airports are operated, social security checks get mailed and we still have our freedoms of speech and assembly. I think our government is a shining example to the world, warts and all. Those countries with religious fundamentalists as leaders and their strict moral codes can't run a county any better than our bunch of misfit derelicts do.

Since we know some politicians are in it for the money and would screw you in a second, why do we allow them to pollute the air waves every October?

I'm mad as hell and I am not going to take it anymore. I'm laying down my remote and watching the only channel without political commercials. I'm watching the Weather Channel. Maybe if everyone watched the Weather Channel, those media moguls who make tons on money every election cycle would see their Neilson Ratings drop to zero. The Advertisers would demand their money back. The Presidents of NBC, CBS, and ABC would get the message and go back to selling Veg-o-matics during the commercial breaks. I don't need more half truths and smears to sway my vote, but I can always use chopped vegetables. I don't need exposure to more stupid political ads at this point in my life; I do need more fiber in my diet.

BEND OVER

—◻—

I have detected a genetic mutation occurring in young people throughout our country. I have made these observations both as an employer of young people and as a father. At first I tried to ignore the problem, thinking it would go away. Next, I compared observations with other employers and parents, hoping what I had observed were isolated cases and not the epidemic I feared. Much to my chagrin, it appears that the last few generations have been born without the "bend over" gene.

When is the last time you saw young folks bend over and pick up a penny on the sidewalk? I have noticed with my own daughter, her inability to bend over and pick clothes off her bedroom floor. Have you been to the bowling alley lately and heard the bowling balls bouncing off the wood as the bowler releases? Young bowlers, who can't bend over enough to release the ball for a smooth transition cause that bounce. Have you seen young people rake leaves or shovel snow lately? First of all, most don't do either, and the ones that do participate in these seasonal exercises to remove nature's unwanted by-products, do so without bending at all. All sorts of electrical and internal combustion devices have been invented so one does not have to bend over at all. I'm telling you it is an epidemic; we must do something about this situation.

If you go back just a few years, to my fathers' generation, they spent half their lives bent over. My father dropped out of school during the depression to go work on a horse farm and earn money to help keep the family farm from being foreclosed. He lived in a bunkhouse Monday through Friday. At four o'clock a.m., he would fall into formation, begin walking, and bend over to pick up rocks and pull weeds. That went on until sundown. On weekends, he would return to the farm and pick blackberries to sell for ten cents a gallon. Picking blackberries and finding bunches the groundhogs missed, takes a great deal of bending over. Bending over saved our family farm.

It is little wonder when I came along; one of my first chores was bending over, pulling weeds in the garden. Our garden was organic, no herbicides or pesticides. I bent over and pinched off leaves of vegetables that had bugs on them in addition to keeping the rows clean.

When I went into the Army, my Platoon Sergeant Sgt. Ricker, was cut from the same cloth as my father. Sgt. Ricker made us fall out into formation at 0 Four Hundred (4:00 a.m.) every morning, dress right and cover down, bend over and walk along policing (clean up) our area. Sgt. Ricker barked out two orders as he stood behind us. "(1) Bend over and pick up anything that God did not put there. (2) all I want to see is A—holes and Elbows, bend over and get to work." The old saying "an Army moves on its stomach" is true. Most of my boot camp was spent in the prone or bent over position.

I have written my congressman to solicit his help in funding a medical study to find a way to combat this "bend over" gene. I suggested that he target the research money to Ohio State, because I have been to my daughter's campus and seen the effects of young people not having the ability to bend over. There are beer cans and little ends of what appear to be home made cigarettes scattered all over the ground after a home football game. I asked my congressman to help clean up of college campuses. His response was that due to the economy; funds are not available, unless I saw fit to contribute to his re-election campaign. I guess that is his way of telling me to "bend over".

EVOLUTION

—◻—

There seems to be a debate going on about whether humans evolved or they were intelligently designed. I think the debate is about the Bible version of the creation of life vs. evolution. It is not a new debate, just a new twist, using bigger words.

Having grown up in the Bible belt, I was taught and believe in the Adam and Eve story in Genesis. I have never questioned that, until recently. Although I find it hard to believe that man just evolved from some cells that crawled out of the seas, I do have some questions about certain people's origin. Could there be two different forms of life?

When I was a kid growing up on our farm, we had a farm hand that helped out with milking and putting up hay from time to time. No one seemed to know where Arthur was from. Uncle Clyde said he was from "overseas". To us kids, overseas meant he was different, although he had two eyes, ten fingers and toes, and seemed a lot like us. He ate weird things like eel and carp we caught on our trout line in the river. We kept the Catfish and the Bass, and saved the strange river animals for Arthur. Add in the fact that Arthur talked funny, maybe he did evolve from the sea.

I went to a clique store in Columbus a while back. The Wild Oats market has lots of organic produce and health food stuff, but the people shopping there are

101

weird. They have lots of body piercings and they eat tofu. I don't think God intended to have us shove pieces of metal through our noses and tongues and I know Jesus would never had tried to feed the multitudes with tofu. So maybe those people evolved from primates who curiously stick things in their orifices. Maybe those people with spiked hair dos and lots of exotic tattoos have some innate animal instinct to try and make their bodies blend in with swamp water? You know, maybe they are instinctively trying to be like the chameleon or gecko?

We just had our county fair. Where do some of those people at the fair come from? I have never seen them at the grocery store or at a restaurant during the course of a year; it's only during fair time that I see them. Where are they the rest of the year? Some of those people roaming around at the fair had more tattoos than they have teeth. How did they come into this world? Do they just come down from the hills once a year? Are they the people that Uncle Clyde told me came from underneath rocks?

I'm afraid I confused my own daughter about creation. When she was eight years old, we traveled to Georgia to watch the birth of a Cabbage Patch Kid in the Babyland Garden Hospital. After a nurse pulled back the cabbage leaves and revealed our newborn doll, complete with adoption papers, how could I explain the birds and the bees? After all, she had watched her doll being delivered just like they showed on the Mattel Toy TV commercials? Telling your kid she came from under a cabbage leaf was a lot easier than trying to explain the mating, sperm, and egg method.

Maybe we have two kinds of origins, just as we have straight or gays, Republicans or Democrats, debit or credit, paper or plastic. Maybe we have people created by the Almighty and people who evolved from a glob that crawled out of the depth of the Oceans, from a garden patch or crawled out from under a rock and came down from the hills.

Whatever you believe you came from, that's OK by me. Myself, I think I am of the intelligent design (made by God); because I get excited about Apple Trees (read the book).

SAVE GAS, STAY HOME

———◻———

We Americans like to travel. It's a right covered in the U.S. Constitution, Article 13, section 101, row 6, seat 13, I think. Americans travel to a theme park once a year for a vacation, where the rides and the hotel are staffed by non-English speaking people. If you have to put up with foreigners while on vacation here in the U.S.A., why not just vacation in a foreign land?

I can give you some travel tips. Thanks to Uncle Sam, I traveled all over Europe. The first thing you need to do is obtain a passport. This is where a lot of Americans go wrong. Women have cheap pictures of themselves made with one color of hair, but when they arrive at a port of entry, like Frankfort Germany, they have a totally different hair color and style. American men never smile for passport photos, so when the customs agents pull them aside, often it is because their photo looks like one of a terrorist or someone wanted for molesting farm animals.

One of the first things to learn in Europe is how to use the bidet in you hotel bathroom. The bidet looks like a horizontal urinal. A bidet is used to clean private parts. There will be no shower in your room because Europeans seldom shower. Add in the fact that their toilet paper is made with pine bark mulch; you must master the bidet or you will have to burn your underwear before entering the United States again.

Paris is the most sophisticated city in all of Europe.

The City Of Lights has thousands of little cars zipping along on their wide avenues and the drivers don't use their cars brakes. They use the horn and hand gestures. Paris has much more to offer than a trip up the Eiffel Tower or a glance at the inspirational stained glass rosette at the Cathedral de Notre Dame. You can also have your pocket picked while waiting in long lines to see the Mona Lisa, you can be pestered at every street corner by a dirty little beggar kid or propositioned by a lady of the night (they come in all shapes, sizes, colors and national origins).

Greece is a wonderful country. Ouzo is served with Ice (few European countries serve ice). The Greek men dance with other men in the night clubs, thereby making their female dates easy pickin' for Americans.

Rome is a romantic place to visit. Toss a coin into Trevi Fountain and watch a dozen or so orphaned boys dive in the water and fight over your penny. Just down the road is The Roman Coliseum where gladiators killed each other while the politicians and their concubines looked on. Kind of like what happens at the NFL Super Bowl now. Then there is the Vatican. The Holy See supports a hoard of street vendors selling tee shirts and little fake marble statues that are made in China.

Switzerland is a refreshing country to visit. Its mountains are pristine, their towns and villages neat and clean. All this is made possible by the income derived from laundering dirty money from the world's dictators and despots.

Germany has 1200 brands of beer and a hundred

types of wurst. Wursts are pig parts and various spices, stuffed into the hog's intestines and eaten with white rad-ishes. The radish assists with the digestion and magni-fies the amount of gas the body produces. Passing gas in large beer halls is a national event in Germany and American soldiers adapt well to that custom

But if you really want to have a good time and save that $4.00 a gallon gas, take this tip…stay home.

Visit Roscoe, The Johnson Humrich Museum, tour the Annin Flag Company and ride your bicycle around Lake Park. There is no place like home.

WHEN IN DOUBT, WHIP IT OUT

—▢—

They caught Old Saddam. Time Magazine made them the subject of their New Year Cover. I sure am proud of our troops. They have been handed a difficult task in Iraq. Our soldiers are like our culture, diversified. They come from cities and farms. They are white or black and every skin color in between. They are poor and some come from families with money, but they all share a commonality. They share a training regiment that starts with boot camp and continues throughout their tour of duty.

The military has a unique way to pound things into your head so many times that when the situation presents itself; soldiers without hesitation recall their training and react accordingly. Training slogans were part of the regiment that imbedded reactions into your mind.

Saddam was alleged to have WMDA's (weapons of mass destruction). Our troops went thru a chemical weapons training program designed to make them automatically don their gas mask at the first hint of a weapon releasing a chemical or biological mist. In training, the slogan was "when in doubt, whip it out". Interpretated "if you are not sure of a gas attack, go ahead and don your gas mask anyway, he who hesitates could be dead"!

"Stay alert – stay alive" was another slogan that was drilled into our heads. We were being made aware of the importance of staying on task, not day dreaming or falling asleep on guard duty.

Slogans also played a role in getting you to sign up to begin your service "Be All You Can Be" that was the slick commercial on TV when I entered the Army. The ad showed a young man trotting the globe having a good time. That ad sure never showed a soldier pulling guard duty on a cold rainy night, or cleaning out the grease trap outside the mess hall.

My friend Bob was in the Marine Corps. Their motto was "We're looking for a few good men". According to Bob they never found any. The marines took what they got, then molded them into what they wanted. My father was in the marines, he said a good DI could make a "silk purse out of a sow's ear".

I have two brothers who served in the Navy. "Let the Journey Begin" was the ad that enticed them to sign up for a four year hitch. They were still waiting for the Journey to Begin after two med curies and a shore duty. Seems pulling watch on a ship bobbing up and down in the ocean was not mentioned by the chief Petty Officer that recruited them. Not seeing land for two months was almost as bad as not seeing their girlfriends for two months also.

"Hurry up and Wait" is a slogan used by all the armed services. It is used to justify getting up at dawn and double time (run) around the parade grounds and then waits for a duce and a half (big truck) to pick you up and move you to the rifle range. There you hurry up, get in the prone position lock and load and then wait for the targets down range to get functional. After qualifying with your weapon and yelling "no brass-no ammo" to the range officer, you double time back to the staging area to wait for noon chow to be scooped up and slapped into your mess kit. Before you get all your food down, you fall into formation so you can hurry up and wait for a weapons inspection. If during inspection you mistakenly called your weapon a "Gun", you had to stand in front of the Platoon and recite this slogan until your drill instructor thought you had it right. "This is my weapon (pointing to your rifle); this is my gun (pointing to your private parts). This is for shooting (Pointing to your weapon); this is for fun (pointing to your private parts). "This is my weapon, this is my gun, this is for shooting, this is for fun", over and over again. Next you hurry up and wait for a truck ride back to the barracks. When you start boot camp, the drill sergeant had a slogan F.T.A. (Fun, Travel, and Adventure). As we approached the end of boot camp, we grunts kept the F.T.A. part, but we changed the meaning to F--- The Army.

I Am From the Government, I Am Here to Help

—◻—

First we had the Cash for Clunkers Automobile Program. Good intentions by our all knowing Federal Government but it had the side effect of driving up the price of the remaining used cars; making it more expensive for entry level working folks to buy a car to drive to work.

We have just completed the Cash for Clunkers Water Heater & Appliance program. Our government incentives did nothing for the new couple just getting a family started. Home owners can buy a $250.00 electric water heater that uses Coal Fired Generated Electricity and receive no rebate; or they could buy a government approved Energy Star fancy natural gas water heater for $900.00 and receive a big fat rebate check from the government. Can you guess which energy lobbyist had a hand in this piece of legislation? Most of the cash incentives went to upper middle class, tree hugger yuppies far from the coal mines of Appalachia.

Congress now is debating Cash for Caulkers incentive program. Again the well off citizens gets $1500.00 for replacing windows, doors, and doing weather stripping projects. Soon, you won't be able to turn on the TV with out some window manufacturing huckster barking out "buy three get one free, no money down, take forever to pay and get a government rebate check.

This "Hat Trick" of give-aways sure will line some one's pockets.

Since rebates and cash incentives seem to be woven into our governmental economic fabric; how about some programs for those of us that have been over looked by our well meaning politicians, might I suggest:

Cash for Bicycles Program: Trade in your K-Mart, Chinese made, piece of road iron they call a bicycle and let the government help you buy a sleek, well engineered, feather light, quality crafted American Made Cannondale or Trek Bicycle.

Cash for Fishing Rod Program: Trade in your cheap Chinese Zebco rod and reel for balanced, graphite, American made Ardent casting reel. With your new rod and reel you can go to Lake Michigan and catch some of those invasive Asian carp that are destroying sport fishing because some bone head government official allowed the carp to be imported into our country.

Cash for BBQ Grills program: Trade in that rusted out charcoal kettle grill made in Taiwan for a new Smoker/Cooker/Steamer Grill entertainment center made in the U.S.A. by Brad Holland and his good ole boys in North Carolina.

Cash for Crappers program: Trade in your old 3.5 gallons of water per flush toilet for one of the new 1.5 gallon water saver toilets that don't work half the time. Just like the Cash for Clunkers program that required your old car to be demolished; this toilet swap program would require you to take a sledge hammer to the old toilet and bust it into a zillion pieces; else your red neck cousin take the old toilet to use as a planter on his front porch.

Cash for Cooler Program: Trade in that cheap Philippine made Styrofoam Igloo cooler for a sleek Stainless Steel, American made Coleman Cooler with 12 volt adapter. With the money the government helps you save, you can fill your new cooler with expensive San Pellegrino imported bottled mineral water and smoke Diplomaticos Cuban cigars with your favorite Washington Politician and dream up other government incentive programs to fit your personal needs.

SCHOOL PROFICIENCY TEST

—▫—

Public Schools, Charter Schools, Parochial Schools, and Home Schooling, all play their role in homogenizing our society. Students from around the world attend our universities. Access to education for all is the single most important factor to the success of our country.

However, education is also our favorite whipping boy. Politicians constantly beat up on our present educational systems. They campaign on the need for better schools and accountability, but don't answer to the same standards. I think politicians, who have to disclose their financial holdings, should also have to disclose their Grade Point Average and ACT scores. Their past academic performance may tone down their rhetoric about education.

I am like most people, a couple of teachers made a profound influence in my life, my 10th grade English Teacher and my Army Boot Camp Drill Sergeant. One taught me to love reading and writing, the other taught me self confidence and perseverance. Both were strict disciplinarians and I felt they were both always picking on me. It wasn't until years after high school and after my honorable discharge, that I realized what they really taught me.

Federal and State mandated Proficency test are attempts to force teachers to teach and students to learn. The problems are (1) good teachers are not made they are born with the ability to disseminate information; (2) tests should be developed by working men and women and not professional educators. I have a problem with any attempt to legislate most things. I've heard legislation described as teaching a pig to dance. It's difficult, not terribly pretty, and really irritates the pig. The abstract academic life does not always translate into real world tests. The tests should not only be a reflection of knowledge gained but also a test of competence in life. The first week of driving a car would not reflect how well you would drive 20 years later. It is just the starting point, showing minimum competence.

I think it is time to measure real world survival skills as well as academic prowess. Like that first week of driving, there are bare minimums that a person should show competence before meeting the big wide world. With this in mind, I suggest high school seniors are able to accomplish the following to qualify for a diploma.

1. Be able to drive a vehicle with a standard transmission (extra points awarded for double clutching).

2. Be able to figure in their head how much change they will receive when tendering a five dollar bill for a $3.21 purchase.

3. Name the four Beatles.

4. Name the 12 Apostles.

5. How to play chess and checkers.

6. Be able to hand write: A. a love letter; B. a letter to the newspaper editor; C. a letter to the IRS explaining why your tax deduction should be allowed.

7. Change a flat tire and change your own oil.

8. Read a tape measure.

9. Equate the moon's phases with regard to best time to fish, plant vegetables, and make love.

10. Be able to identify animal tracks.

11. Identify true north by looking at the moss on a tree trunk.

12. Be able to read a map and a compass.

13. Be able to repair a flush valve and ballcock in a toilet tank.

14. Recite Lincoln's Gettysburg Address.

15. Be able to get out off bed and be at work on time, without the use of an alarm clock.

16. Turn all lights off when leaving a room.

17. Do your own laundry.

18. Remember Mothers Day and send her a card, no matter where you are.

Of course, I guess this all goes back to home. I know Grandmother certainly had that list as the bare minimum before I could leave the farm. Maybe Grandmother was just ahead of the curve. Or maybe the Legislators are way behind the curve. Perhaps those dancing pigs just won't get any prettier.

SCROOGENOMICS

—▣—

My family hosted a Japanese exchange student a few years back. After attending a Christmas candle lighting ceremony at Roscoe Village, a friend asked Mariko how an American Christmas compared with Christmas in Japan. Markio said her family bought inexpensive gifts for immediate family members and they only shopped the last week before the holiday. Mariko went on to say she notice Christmas advertising and shopping when she stepped off the plane and into the airport in Columbus, Ohio when she first arrived in America back in August.

That pretty well sums up my belief that Yuletide in America has gotten out of hand.

As a kid growing up on a farm, I remember getting up Christmas day and milking before we opened our gifts. I remember gifts of a brick of 22 long rifle shells, new underwear and socks, a bag of chocolate drops and bananas and oranges for the whole family. We would have a big dinner with home grown, homemade everything including a free range big fat hen from our chicken coop. I remember the chocolate drops the most. Isn't it funny I can remember gifts of over 50 years ago, yet I am hard pressed to remember gifts I got last year?

Today Christmas gift spending in America is over 66 billion dollars according to a noted economist at the Wharton Business School at the University of Pennsylvania. Professor Joel Waldfogel wrote a book titled

"Scroogeonomics" which my daughter bought me because the title fits my personality. The professor shares my thoughts about the demise of the meaning of Christmas and makes suggestions on how to buy Christmas gifts of value using economic sense and thus ending the advanced decadence of our past giving habits. Reference the Chia Pet, Snuggie blanket, Black and Decker Snake Light, Bass-O-Matic and all the other goofy gifts that flood the air waves during the holidays.

I have taken the lessons of Scroogenomics to heart and might I suggest the following to Tribune readers so they too can be good givers of value this holiday season:

An American Flag made by Annin Company of Coshocton. Sewn by good looking ladies and not imported from some Far East sweat shop employing children. A case of shotgun shells from Woodbury Outfitters or Richcreek's Hardware. Get your bullets while you can before Nancy Pelosi and her left coast friends make them illegal to buy. A La-Z-Boy recliner; next to a dog, a recliner is man's best friend. A beauty make over for your wife at a local Hair Salon; what better gift for you and your wife, a gift certificate for a new woman? For the person that has everything, don't get them anything! If you want to show them respect, make a donation in their name to Hospice or the Red Cross or any charity. There are many other good value gifts from merchant's right here in our county. You could discover them in less time than it would take to drive to Columbus or Heath, fight the traffic, get a driving violation ticket from a hidden traffic camera and find a parking space. Stay at home this Holiday season. After all the only two things in life that are certain, is death and taxes. Why not shop where you pay property taxes and where you own a cemetery plot?

CADENCE

As my wife and I watched the news the other evening, a segment aired about young men and women signing up for military service. The clip included a platoon of troops double timing (running) and calling out cadence. I told my wife that was my fondest memory of the Army, falling out for PT run (physical training).

"What's this cadence thing?" she asked. "Are you singing or yelling and what are you saying?" Cadence is something like rap today. Cadence has to rhyme and tell a story. Common themes for the story are the girl back home or what you plan on doing during your next weekend pass off the Army Base. You call out cadence to make sure everyone is "in step". It takes your mind off the physical exhaustion. Calling cadence was what got most of us through the rigors of Airborne School. A lot of cadences were "Jody calls". Jody was the guy back home that got out of the draft because he had flat feet, but now he was asking out the girl you left behind.

Ain't no use in going home;
Jody's got your girl and gone.
Ain't no use in feeling blue;
Jody's got your sister, too.
Ain't no use in looking' back;
Jody's got your Cadillac...

Left, Right, Left, Right

Mama, Mama, can't you see?

O, What the Army's done to me…

They sat me down in the chair,

When I looked I had no hair.

Oh, mama I want to go home…

Left, Right, Left, Right

You were not allowed to drop out of a run in Airborne School. If you did, you were "washed out" and sent to a non-combat unit. I had a bunk buddy from Toledo that wanted to drop out every morning because he had been out all night in the go-go bars off base. The Jody calls "kept" him going until he sweated out all the long neck beers, then he was good to go for the rest of the day.

A lot of the guys "bitched" about the PT, the food, the beds, and the latrine. I thought the accommodations were pretty good. The forced marches were no further than I had to go to sell eggs at the Pascal General Store down the lane from our farm. The "C" rations were a little bland, but a little G.I. Gourmet Sauce (Tabasco), dried onion, and garlic salt could turn the Army's canned meat products into a gastronomic delight. The mess hall food was almost like farm food, real butter, real milk, real mashed potatoes, real eggs, and things cooked in lard. Some mess sergeants could give Betty Crocker or my Grandmother a run for their money when it came to baking pies.

The beds, well, sleeping in a room with 40 other men

is a little different than sleeping in one room with my three brothers, but it did have its good points. Sitting on your bunk, with "lights out", a blanket over your head, reading a letter from your girl back home for the fourth time was a little lonely, but sharing homemade cookies and candy sent by moms from all over the U.S.A. was a smorgasbord of regional confectionaries. It was an experience sitting on your foot locker; spit shining your boots and talking to a guy from a town whose population was bigger than your whole home state (New York City). It broadened your horizons scrubbing the floor with a tooth brush with a guy whose English is a second language (Latino). You shared pictures of that special girl, or your hot wheels (car), high school prom, your back home hang out, your family.

City boys didn't like the latrine (bathroom). I grew up with three brothers and a two holer outhouse, so using the Army latrine with no partitions between 10 toilets was no big deal. Some city boys were a little constipated for a while until they got used to sitting down together. It was the same with the showers, one shower room, 10 shower heads, and no partitions. I had been skinny dipping in ponds and creeks since I was 5, so lathering up with 9 other guys was a good way to catch up on what you did the night before…Left, Right, Left, Right.

THE GREENS STAMP ACT

———□———

Ah, spring is in the air. With spring comes the availability of one of my favorite foods, dandelion greens.

Greens were a major staple for farm meals. Dandelion Greens were the first to pop out of the ground following winter's hold on the earth. Dandelions were followed by Poke Salet, then Turnip Greens, Mustard Greens, Kale Greens, and Collard Greens.

We prepared our dandelion greens two ways. First, like spinach, cooked with a little jowl bacon, onions, garlic, salt, and pepper. Second, we wilted the dandelion greens with hot bacon grease, green onions, a little apple vinegar and sugar.

My Aunt Buehla would visit from the city from time to time and she always brought grocery store bought food with her (she didn't like poor people food we ate). She brought Iceberg Lettuce once. My Grandmother made a salad with her lettuce, but added our home grown onions, tomatoes, radishes, mangos, and some tender green dandelion leaves. She thought the dandelions were endive.

The bright yellow flowers had a major role in my early romances. A necklace made of dandelion flowers given to my first girlfriend, an important gesture of courtship. Once the blossoms turned to seed, I would blow the puff ball and help the wind sow the seeds, while I was trying to sow my own seeds by talking Carolyn Lynn into going up into the hayloft to play doctor and nurse.

Grandfather said the honey made in early spring was the best because the bees gathered nectar from the yellow dandelion flowers. Grandfather used the dandelion flower to forecast the weather. If the yellow flower did not fold up at dusk, he said that meant it would rain the next day. Our hogs loved to eat dandelions, but the mules wouldn't touch them. All farmers know that the pig is the smartest farm animal and that horses and mules are the dumbest. Uncle Clyde ate dandelion greens because they are an herbal remedy for a sluggish liver caused by heavy drinking. That's ironic because Uncle Clyde made home made wine from dandelions too.

"Dent de lion" is the French word meaning "lions tooth". The French are credited with naming this eatable weed because to them the jagged edge leaves looked like the teeth in a lion's mouth. The French have a knack for making a common food sound like a culinary romantic encounter. Truffles (Mushrooms), pate de foie gras (Goose Liver), Fromage de la tete de porta (Head Cheese) see what I mean?

There is an Annual Dandelion Cook Off Festival May 6th in Dover, Ohio. It is a family fun day dedicated to the fine foods and wines made from the yellow weed. The festival includes a 5K run. I think that got started because one who eats too many dandelion greens get the "runs" and they need to be in good physical shape in order to make it to the outhouse before having an accident. I am entering a recipe for pierogi stuffed with dandelion greens and onions. I also have a dandelion greens and goat cheese bruschetta I would like to enter as well.

Many of you spend lots of money every spring on herbicides to eradicate dandelions from your lawn. You also pay very high sales tax to the state of Ohio to support, among other worthless government programs, your tax dollars goes to support the food stamp giveaway.

I propose we stop issuing food stamps during the dandelion growing season. Instead the state would issue dandelion picking vouchers. The vouchers would allow those on the dole to come in our yards, uproot the dandelions, take them home and eat them. Under this program tax payers will have beautiful, chemical free lawns, and voucher clients would learn a little about work and get some exercise.

This environmental friendly proposal to handle two pests (dandelions and free loaders), makes so much common sense, I am sure our do gooder legislators will quickly pass the necessary laws. It could be listed in the Ohio Revised Code as the "Greens Stamp Act".

SOMEBODY HAS TO BE AT FAULT

—◻—

I've mentioned my Grandmother often in this column. She was many things to our little family. She was an iron fist in a velvet glove. She was the moral compass to guide us, the foreman to get the job of the farm done, a teacher, and of course, the finest cook on the earth. I think the cooking ability led to the other skills. I remember fondly how she could take humble ingredients and fashion fine farm cuisine. Similarly, I admired the way she could cut through layers and get to the core of a subject. Her way was homespun, but often right on the money.

In watching the news lately, it seems everyone is blaming someone else for anything that goes wrong. There seems to be a script. Something goes wrong, and the game of pinning the decision on someone else starts. No matter what, there are few statesmen and many politicians involved in most of these situations. The FBI blames the Justice department, the Pentagon blames the CIA, the President blames the Congress, and Washington blames it all on us, the unwashed huddled masses. The Beltway around Washington is the dam holding back the blame. No one seems to want to get hit with the splash of notoriety that inevitably follows the latest Washington fiasco. I guess we have too many dam politicians holding back the blame...

Grandmother always said "Someone has to be at

fault!" Perhaps it was the simpler times, or the simplicity of farm life, but Grandmother could cut to the heart of the matter. It was a black and white world, and there were innocent and guilty. If you were innocent, the Good Book would put you in good company. If you were guilty, it was time to stand up and take the punishment. I learned this lesson more than once. Grandmother would send me to the Willow tree for a switch. In fact I cut so many switches I thought Grandmother was an Electrician. Mostly after some adventure, Bobby Ray and I would be hauled in front of Grandmother. She was judge, jury and executioner. She would give us a steely look, draw herself up to her full height, and dole out the punishment in a swift and sure manner. Sometimes Bobby Ray started it, sometimes it was me. No matter who, Grandmother figured she was just making up for a previous missed opportunity. Although we tried hard, we were overmatched. Grandmother had been dealing with Uncle Clyde for years. Bobby Ray and I could not come close to Uncle Clyde's efforts to shed blame.

This brings us back to the news. I think it would be bad for reelection, but good for the nation if Washington had a Grandmother policy. Instead of passing the blame, it would be time to stand up and be accountable. "Yes I did it!" would be the rallying cry. There would be no need for spin doctors, public relations firms or lobbyists. This alone could drop the population of the metropolitan D.C. area just from that one move. There would be no need for congressional hearings, ethics committees, and confessional traffic would drop. Aside from those benefits, there may be a resulting change in philosophy. The sharpening of decision making skills would be a definite result of this whole concept. Grandmother would be glad to say,"I did it!"

Of course, there is always a down side to any issue. As Uncle Clyde used to say, "I don't want to chase the mice out of the barn; they might like the house better!" Maybe keeping all those folks inside the Beltway is the best choice. I always thought Uncle Clyde was just avoiding the work, but again he was ahead of the curve. He was just keeping the nuisance in one place, not avoiding. For that he'd probably say," Yes, I did it!"

HAND GUNS

Go ahead, make my day!

The State of Ohio seems to be leading the nation in new laws. First Ohio enacted a concealed gun law. Now, Columbus has passed laws banning smoking in all public places including Bars and Restaurants. It seems some folks don't have enough to worry about. Back home we called them busy bodies. Some times busy bodies get elected to public office, and then we call them politicians. Politicians are under the gun by smokers and gun carriers. Each side has their gripes about both laws, and I think it is time we used one law to enforce the other law.

Let me begin by saying I am an ex-smoker. I grew up on a Tobacco farm and was rolling my own by age 12. My talent to roll smooth, even cigarettes came in handy later in the 60's at fraternity parties. College women like guys who could roll a sleek ez wider. Our nation's capital Rotanda has a motif of corn, wheat, and tobacco; it signifies our National heritage. I enjoyed the NASCAR races when they were called the Winston Cup. I enjoyed Television shows like Ed Sullivan, Red Skelton and Jack Benny which were brought to us by cigarettes makers Chesterfield, Pall Mall, Salem and Viceroy. I can't imagine going to a Stones or Alice Cooper concert with out smoking. Even the hoe downs in the neighbors' barn would not have been the same without longnecks and ready rolls. But, things change. My daughter asked me to quit smoking. It was the hardest thing I ever did; but in hindsight, the concealed gun law could have helped me kick butts sooner.

I am a firm believer in the right to bear arms. I had my own rifle by the time I started smoking (age 12). My 22 caliber, single shot, bolt action Savage was used to put many a meal on the table (squirrel and rabbit). When I turned 16, I received my father's 16 gauge double barrel Remington shot gun. With a shot gun I brought home a mess of Quail or Doves for the family supper table. In the Army I qualified as a sharp shooter with the M16 rifle, M79 grenade launcher and the 45 automatic pistols. My M113A1 Armored Personal Carrier had "old granddad", a 50 caliber machine gun. I was schooled in how to call in 155 mm artillery support, how to call for F4 Phantom (Air Force Jet) close in fire support and although I never had the opportunity to use the training, I could have asked for 16 inch naval gun support from the U.S.S. Missouri Battleship. All my role models growing up carried guns. The Lone Ranger, the legend of Davey Crockett, and Daniel Boone, John Wayne, and Hop along Cassidy.

But times change. Smoking is not good for you. Non-smokers don't want to be around smokers and suck in second hand smoke. We have deemed guns dangerous, so we want to conceal them (figure that one out).

Since some people are hell bent on carrying a gun and they are not proud enough to have it out in the open, strapped to their side the way God intended; and some people are hell bent on smoking in prohibited areas, allow conceal gun toters to shoot illegal smokers. If you are sitting in a Bob Evans after church with your family and you see a lady light up a Virginia Slim in the next booth, stand up and shoot. With the first shot, aim at the cigarette, chances are she will stop inhaling (toking for you of the 60's generation). If she doesn't snuff out her smoke, then go ahead "make your day".

By combining the two laws we give incentives to smokers to quit and we fulfill the concealed gun toters dream to play Dirty Harry. A win-win situation.

YAK DUNG

—◻—

I took off from work early the other day and went home. It was past noon, but "nooner" was on my mind. At home my wife was watching Oprah on TV. Viewing the Queen of Talk, pretty well takes a woman's thoughts away from any afternoon delight. I knew I didn't want to sit and watch Oprah with my wife, because Dr. Phil would come out and start talking about how dumb men are. Dr. Phil would work the audience and the home viewers in a frenzy of male bashing. Next thing, my wife would start in on me for not fixing the dripping kitchen faucet, for being insensitive, for forgetting our anniversary, for keeping the TV remote and all the other bad habits I have. As I was getting up to leave the room Oprah starts talking about Yak Dung.

The Oprah show this day featured the adventures of an Atlanta couple who lived with a Mongolian family for a couple of weeks. Being immersed into this Chinese culture meant living in a tent, eating sheep parts and drinking fermented Yak milk. The modern American family adjusted well to their new environment except for one thing. The Mongolians collect the Yak Dung, dry it and then use it for fuel in the stove to cook their meals. Oprah was fixated on collecting and burning Yak poop. Oprah kept saying how disgusting all this poop was.

"What's the big deal", I asked my wife. "Everyday in the hardware store, we fix peoples' toilets. That's what

131

pays the bills!" I have been around lots of poop in my life, and I think it made me a better man. As she rolled her eyes, I began to tell her of my first recollections with poop.

I marveled at watching my grandmother empty the poop deposits from the Thunder Mug (combinet) every morning. She was a petite woman, but she could fling poop as if she were a female Russian shot putter on steroids. Grandmother could always land the contents in the weeds beside the chicken coop. That made the chickens have to hunt.

As a preteen, I earned a little money from time to time helping neighbors clean out their W.P.A. outhouses or helping dig new ones. We didn't collect cow dung out in the pasture, but I sure stepped in plenty of cow patties barefooted as I frolicked thru the fields trying to catch grasshoppers for fishing bait. We did fork out straw and manure from the barn and spread it on the garden. I caught pigs for a Veterinarian and had pig poop permeate my skin. I worked on my university's dairy research farm while in college. My job was to repair and maintain the conveyor that took the cow manure from the milking parlor to the manure pond. In the Army we mixed the poop in the latrines with diesel fuel and burned it.

My best poop experience was in Germany. The little village just outside the military base I lived in was known for the prize cabbage they grew. Der Kopfkohl (cabbage heads) grew as big as basketballs. At harvest time, pitch forks were used to spear the heads and toss them into a hay wagon for the ride to the kraut factory.

We grew cabbage in our garden on the farm, but nothing near the size of these. I often wondered what their growing secret was. One day as I topped the hill of the street leading to my apartment, there was a pungent smell and almost a brown mist floating over the valley where the cabbage grew.

I asked my landlord, Herr Weit what was going on? "Der Jauchegrube Tag", he explained. The day all the village septic tanks are emptied and sprayed on the cabbage fields.

"Are you finished" my wife said in discuss? "Yes, I said. Oh by the way what's for supper", I asked. "Cabbage Rolls", she said.

BEST FATHER'S DAY GIFT, EVER!

—◻—

Being a father is one of the most important jobs one can ever have. From the time my wife said "I'm pregnant!" my life has been filled with uncertainties, an occasional disappointment, but mostly pride and happiness.

It all started in the hospital delivery room. Unlike the old days when my father smoked cigars and sipped whiskey in the father's waiting room, I was prepared. I attended Lamaze classes, I went in with my wife for her pre-natal doctor visits, I read magazine articles and pamphlets on birthing. I trained to be a new father. After all, I have watched and helped deliver calves and pigs on the farm. Helping with my own child's birth couldn't be much different.

When my wife's water broke, I came apart. All that training vanished from my mind and all I could think about was getting to the hospital as fast as I could and getting this nine month ordeal over with. The labor room was hot, cramped and I was hungry. The breathing techniques and pushing exercises seemed like a waste of time. My wife was getting grouchy. The nurses were encouraging my wife by saying, "It won't be long now". But the nurses pretty much ignored me.

The trip down the hallway to the delivery room took forever it seemed. The doctor walked in nonchalantly speaking with the anesthesiologist about their morning golf game. Did the doctor not realize the importance of this event?

The next few minutes were a blur. The team of doctors and nurses performed like a NASCAR pit crew. Orders were given, instruments were handed, and towels were placed. It was organized chaos.

My blurred vision came into sharp focus as the nurse wrapped the crying baby girl in a blanket and handed her to me.

I always thought all babies looked the same, but not my daughter. My daughter was the most beautiful child I have ever seen.

Thus began my journey into fatherhood.

The next 26 years went by very fast, but I remember the milestones as if they were yesterday:

There were the diapers to the big girl pants potty training period.

There was the tearful, first day on the school bus episode.

Elementary school graduation was especially gratifying for me because my daughter was recognized as the winner of the Geography Bee. The Geography Bee was one of the few homework assignments I was smart enough to play a major role in helping.

Then there was the "birds and the bees" sex talk. I still break out in a cold sweat when thinking about that one.

First date went by fairly easily, much better than the first Prom. I guess I remember what I did on my first

Prom. Surely my daughter wouldn't....

Memories of High School Graduation were still fresh in my mind when along came the College commencement. Now all those years of worrying are over. CD's, Savings Bonds, and Savings Accounts are all depleted, but my little girl is a modern woman with an education and a job!

And what did my little pride and joy do with one of her first pay checks? She bought her father a much needed watch for Fathers Day. That was the best fathers day gift ever; one that she did not charge to my credit card.

ALL THAT GLITTERS IS NOT GOLD

I see my Ohio Worker's Compensation Premium has taken a hefty increase, again. I also see some of the money I pay into this fund is missing or is invested in questionable securities. There is a big fuss over the fact that Workers Comp. funds were invested in rare coins. Some of the coins are missing and many are not worth what they paid for them. The investment advisor just happened to be a major political donor. This guy was also being paid by the State for serving on a couple state controlling boards. This old boy was caught red handed with his hand in the cookie jar. It seems that when good people leave home for Columbus or Washington, they are like little kids away from home the first time, they do dumb things.

My Uncle Clyde always said, "All that glitters, is not gold." Uncle Clyde learned that truth the hard way, by losing money on "shiny" investment schemes during the Laissez-faire, free market policies in the 1930's. Some of Uncle Clyde's holdings included the Studebaker Automobile Corporation; Green River Railroad Company, and the Bradley Aircraft Company. Never heard of them? That's because all went belly up.

The Great Depression taught a whole generation that there is no such thing as easy money. Unfortunately we have many today that have not learned that lesson. Greed and corruption has raised its ugly head in American Corporations and in Politics, time and time again.

It does not have to be this way. We can stop these cycles of unethical behavior, followed by indictments and bankruptcy. We just have to adopt a few simple rules for politicians and CEO's.

Rule #1: Politicians could not live in Columbus or Washington. Politicians would have to live in their district 9 months out of the year and look us in the eye when they are grocery shopping or dispensing gasoline in their cars. For 3 months out of the year they would live in Army barracks in the evening and work in the Capital or State House during the day. There would be a bed check and lights out at 11 o'clock in their barracks. No cocktail parties hosted by lobbyists. Food would be served in a mess hall setting and could consist of American Food that "sticks to your ribs." No more Chateaubriand and Caviar chased by Champagne. Air Travel to and from the Legislators' home towns would be handled by the U.S. Air Force M.A.C. (Military Airlift Command). The M.A.C. C130 cargo planes can take off and land anywhere. They could land at Coshocton's Airport or just a straight stretch on any county road. Granted, M.A.C. planes are not quite full of "creature comforts". M.A.C. planes have web sling seats and are so noisy you must wear ear plugs, but the vibrations and turbulence make you appreciate the good earth, when you land. They were good enough to haul me around when I was in the military; they are good enough for politicians.

Rule #2: All CEO's and CFO's would have to work their way up through the ranks and would have to show they had hard labor type summer jobs while helping their parents pay their way through college. Calluses and scars must be part of their anatomy. Corporate jets would be banned with the preferred method of travel being coach class, commercial airlines. No reserved parking spaces in parking lots. Let them hike in if they arrive last. No executive bathrooms. After all, you can learn a lot about your company in the employee bathroom. You make your own coffee and take you own phone calls. All employees and retirees are paid before the CEO can cash his or her check. Three martini dinners would be replaced by Burgers, Jack Daniels, and Beer Nuts.

These 2 simple rules would rein in folks who my Grandmother would describe as "Being too big for their britches." Grandmother had a knack for keeping it simple and getting it right.

THAT IS NOT A HICKEY
ON MY NECK!

—⬡—

I feel very fortunate in that I have a job I enjoy going to every day. It's a good thing too, because my wife certainly doesn't need me under foot all day. She likes that I work a lot. I have been in the retail hardware business now for 25 years. Every day is a challenge, every day something different happens. The community has been good to me, and hopefully I have filled a need. I certainly enjoy a good laugh now and again and I am not afraid to laugh at myself. Most of my laughs come from me or one of my customers doing something dumb.

A young lady bought a Pet Safe Radio Fence from our store the other day. She wanted to install it herself while her husband was away on a fishing trip to Canada. Her family had recently moved from a farm to a house on a busy street in town. The family Collie was not adjusting well to being tied up. The Pet Safe Fence would allow the Collie some freedom to romp and run without getting into traffic.

This lady called me the next day to say something was wrong. Her Collie just walked over the cable she had buried around her yard. The dog should have received a powerful electrical shock on his neck from the collar as he approached the buried boundary, marked with little flags. The flags would give the dog references until he was conditioned to know where to stop.

I asked the lady to get out her owner's manual and we would walk through the trouble shooting guide. The first item was, check batteries in shock collar. "Oh, the batteries are new and they really work." my customer told me. "Did you test them with an electrical multi meter?" I asked. "My husband has several meters in his work shop, he works for the Power Company; but no, I did not test the batteries that way." she told me. "Well, how do you know the batteries are good?" I asked. "I put the shock collar around my own neck and I walked across the cable I buried and I got one hell of a jolt, that's how I know the batteries are good!" she barked.

I could tell she was beside herself and I could hear a baby crying in the background.

I told her we had an employee going by her house on the way to deliver a bath tub that afternoon and that he would bring longer collar spikes with him, because the second item on the trouble shooting guide was to "replace spikes if your dog has long hair such as Collies". The longer spikes did the trick. My employee said the lady was searing a scarf around her neck as if hiding her red badge of courage.

The lady called to say thanks the next day, and said she was sorry if she had sounded angry. I told her we stand behind the products we sell, but for what it's worth, always read and follow the owner's manual and trouble shooting guide when working with something new. She said her husband never reads instructions and she should have known better. "Sorry, I acted like a man." she said.

Funny things happen in other ACE Hardware stores

141

all across this great land of ours. My friend, JR from Villas, N.J. sent me the following story:

A customer walks in the store carrying a homing pigeon. Apparently, the little fellow had its foot taken off in some strange homing pigeon accident. He was quite the "champion of homing pigeons" in our area, and the owner wanted to keep the little guy's royal bloodline going for a few more generations. The customer asked me for ideas on how the pigeon could continue to mount his mates; you know have his way with the ladies. After some careful thought and planning, I came up with a yellow plastic drywall anchor "prosthesis", super glued in place. The hardware store surgery worked, the pigeon went on to father many more offspring.

FORD TRACTOR

—⊡—

Henry Ford built Model T's to get horses off the streets and built tractors to get horses out of the field. Henry called his first tractor an "Automobile Plow".

Today's tractors with air conditioned closed cabs, CD players, GPS hands off control steering, and air ride seats are a far cry from our old 9N Ford, which was the first in our family and the first on our lane.

As with anything new, neighbors and family members were nosy. How much did it cost? Why did you buy a Ford instead of a Farmall? Who bought your team of mules? What did they fetch? Uncle Clyde knew everyone was jealous. Uncle Clyde pulled a Tom Sawyer on us. "How would you like to take her for a spin? Go ahead, try that bottom plow alongside the creek." he would say. Next thing we knew, Uncle Clyde was holding court telling stories and a neighbor was doing the plowing on the cornfield. "Like it? Doesn't it pull that plow so smooth? There's no jerking around like with the mules. Go ahead; take her for a few more rows."

I was ten when Uncle Clyde bought that tractor. He let me drive about anywhere I wanted so long as I stayed off State Roads. Kenny Chesney had a country music hit song titled "She thinks my tractor's sexy, it really turns her on." I always felt like a man in control when I was on a tractor. If I was sent to the mill for feed I always took the long way back so I could drive past my heart throb,

Carolyn Lynn's farm. When I was a little older (age 12) and was smoking, I always stopped at her house to light up a Pall Mall.

Ten years later, I still had that "Macho" feeling, not on a farm tractor, but in my M113A1 Army Armored Personnel Carrier rolling along the sugar beet fields looking for young German maidens while we were supposed to be training for the war game scenario of the Russian invasion from Czechoslovakia.

The Ford had a clutch and brake on the left side which took some getting used to and there was no gas peddle, rather a throttle on the steering column. The spring steel perforated seat for me was like putting my little 10 year old butt in a wash tub, I sloshed around in that big seat, so I always drove standing up. Uncle Clyde on the other hand, his "big lard butt" as grandmother referred to, seemed well suited for the wide bodied seat.

The Ford had a three point hitch designed by Harry Ferguson. With the hydraulics, this hitch made it easy even for a kid to hook up an implement, wagon, or plow and go.

Uncle Clyde liked Henry Ford, but said old Henry screwed (money wise) Old Harry Ferguson out of his three point hitch invention. Uncle Clyde also liked Old Louis Hupp. Louis and his brother Robert built cars in Cleveland to compete with Henry Fords cars. Uncle Clyde owned a Hupp at one time and even bought some shares of stock in the Hupp Motor Car Corporation.

Uncle Clyde's Hupp disappeared while he was away in the Army in WWII. Grandmother said something about it being confiscated in lieu of non-payment for services rendered by a woman he left behind. Uncle Clyde gave me his shares of Hupp Motors, so I could cash them in and retire early. That's one reason why I still have to work every day and have hobbies that don't cost any money, like riding a bicycle or writing smart aleck stories (as my wife refers to my scribblings). Hupp shares are no longer listed on the New York Stock Exchange. Now they are only traded on e-bay (listed under worthless collectibles). I wish Uncle Clyde had given me that Old 9N Ford instead.

CEREAL KILLERS ON THE LOOSE

—▫—

I miss lots of things from my youth. One of the traditions I miss since leaving the farm is a big homemade breakfast. I thought I would try to pass on this tradition to my daughter this Christmas. I decided to make our family a real down home Christmas breakfast.

I started out by frying in lard some fresh brown eggs I bought from the Amish. Next came fried Goetta and some Scrapple, followed by a slice of country ham and red-eye gravy. My made from scratch buttermilk biscuits came out of the oven just in time to be used to sop up anything runny on the plate (egg yolks and gravy). To really turn this in to a lip smacking feast, I sliced a piece of Head Cheese and some Souse. What would have made the breakfast even more authentic would have been some raw milk from Mr. Richardson's herd of Brown Swiss cows, some home churned butter and real cream for my coffee. My daughter turned up her nose, said I stunk up the kitchen, and said this type of food was not good for me.

Not to let this college kid (who is still wet behind the ears) get the best of me, I went into one of my "When I was a boy" speeches. "When I was growing up," I started, "We lived close to the land."

We grew our own food or swapped for food with a neighbor we knew." I was on a roll now. "Now my city cousins bought food at grocery stores that stocked food made in factories. These food factories, in order to compete with one another, found ways to cut cost and make a cheaper product. These adulterated products had cheap additives like cereal fillers and were whipped to add air; thereby making more volume and hence more profits."

"My grandfather said he used this method during the great depression to make feed for his team of mules. Grandfather mixed sweet molasses with saw dust to make a cheap feed, which the mules ate and were too dumb to know better. Uncle Clyde said Mr. Hormel started that deceitful practice with people food when he started the canned spiced ham product, SPAM (SP from Spiced, AM from Ham, SPAM). Mr. Hormel also got a big fat government contract for his military version in WWII, Canned Ham and Lima Beans. Ironically, Spam is a delicacy in Hawaii to this day!"

I saw my daughter roll her eyes, so I decided to get off my soap box and ask her to compare ingredients with me, her food vs. my country food. Her Nutri-Grain Breakfast Bar contains: flour, high fructose corn syrup, artificial flavor, wheat starch, and partially hydrogenated soybean oil among other things I can't pronounce. My scrapple contains: pork, cornmeal, broth, spices, pepper and nutmeg.

Her Special K cereal contains: wheat gluten, sugar, defatted wheat germ, salt, high fructose corn syrup, dried whey, malt flavoring, and calcium caseinate among other things. My Goetta contains pork and beef parts, pinhead oats, pepper and spices. Her margarine spread contains: soybean oil, whey, emulsifiers, monoglycerides, potassium sorbate, sodium benzoate and other chemicals. My butter contains butter.

"I see your point, she said, but what about that Head Cheese, the name just makes me sick." She said "Do you recall eating goose liver when you were on your high school trip to France?" I asked. "No, that sounds disgusting, too." she said. "How about Pate de foie gras?" "Yes, that was an excellent appetizer we had at a French Bistro.

"Ok, Head Cheese in French is Fromage de la tete de pora, sound better?" "Yes, that sounds continental, sophisticated and expensive, I think I will try a bite now that it has a fancy name." she said.

I wonder what grandfather named the molasses and sawdust mixture, to get the mules to like it so well. Maybe he should have called it Pate de Hormel.

GET A LOOK AT THEM
CITY SLICKERS

—▫—

I have lived and worked in cities every since I left the farm. Cities as big as Chicago, London or Munich and as small as Coshocton. All cities have amenities like municipal water, sewers, paved streets, delivered newspaper or police protection which are comforting and give me a feeling of security. Throw in pizza shops and gas stations that sell coffee on every corner, a good library and convenience stores that sell lottery tickets, city life is good.

I have grown to love the hustle and bustle of city life and I love my city neighbors. However, there are things about city folks that I just don't understand. Take for instance their dogs and cats. On the farm we always had cats and a litter or two of kittens around. They were there to keep mice out of the corn crib, moles out of the garden and snakes off of the front porch. We never fed the cats, except once in awhile Uncle Clyde would squirt a little milk from a cow's teat toward one of the cats while milking, just to drive the cats crazy. We never named the cats; they were just around, probably doing what they did at the beginning of time. We never messed with the cats, except once during squirrel hunting season a cat got up in a hickory nut tree and the light of dawn made it's tail look bushy...

City folks have cats in their house and feed them

expensive meats from little round tin cans. This canned cat meat looks, smells and probably taste better than the canned meat in my Army C-Rations. City folks spend good money on cat litter, kitty toys and they have exotic names like Sabrina or Chantilly for their cats.

As far as dogs, we had an old mongrel, Blackie. Blackie and I grew up together. When I was just a little fella, I was not allowed off the farm unless Blackie went with me. I could walk to the Pascal General Store to sell eggs or to fish in Mr. Richardson's pond if Blackie tagged along. My grandmother knew I wouldn't get lost with Blackie by my side and if I got hurt, Blackie could go for help. Blackie was fed table scraps. Blackie knew better than to steal eggs out of the hen house, but he occasionally stumbled on some duck eggs along a fence row on the backside of the farm and it was ok to suck the wild eggs. He slept on the front porch, but would wake up in the middle of the night to chase coons out of the garden. Blackie and I swam in creeks and ponds together, jumped in the hayloft together and herded cows together. When I grew to become a teenager, Blackie would serve as a guard while I was jumping in the hayloft with my heart throb, Carol Lynn.

City folks let their dogs sleep… in their bedrooms. City dogs eat special foods that are nutritional and make their stool the correct texture and stiffness so as to allow their owners to pick up the poop easily and deposit into a baggie. City dogs go to the hair dresser and ride in their owners' cars. City dogs seem to only come in two sizes, tiny and huge. Tiny dogs have sissy names like Fifi or Champagne and their owners kiss them on the mouth (country boys' only kiss women). Huge dogs have names like Brute or Amazon and their owners' household furnishings are all chewed up. Their cars have dog slobbers all over the windows.

Some city folks have life styles that don't lend themselves to taking care of dogs and cats. They have pets that demand less attention. My daughter is one of those busy young educated urbanites. Fish, rabbits, turtles, frogs or even doves and other birds are popular among the young hip "generation x" city folks. I hunted and ate all of those animals growing up on the farm. Maybe that is why my daughter never invites me along to her friends' houses.

Aunt Nora's Pool Hall and the Ball and Cue

—☐—

Summertime the doors were propped open, front and back. This helped a breeze blowing through to suck out the cigarette smoke. Everyone smoked. A few old timers were rolling their own from a cloth sack of Bull Durham and some papers. Most boys were smoking ready-mades, unfiltered Pall Malls, and Lucky Strikes. Girls seemed to prefer filtered Kools.

Six pool tables in different states of disrepair and one hustler table, the one where the real money was played for, filled the room. Beer signs, some lit with neon lights, lined the walls. Sterling, Hudepol, Falls City, Wiedemann and Carling Black Label were the brews of the age. Tobacco signs were everywhere also. Viceroy, Raleigh, Chesterfield, Redman, and Mule Days had signs showing the glamour of the wicked weed. A small bar at the rear served only long necks and you needed a "church key" to open one. The bar maid wore a white shirt tied at the waist and short shorts. She would show a little cleavage too, it help sell more beer. Our county was "dry", but seems the local authorities turned their head when it came to Aunt Nora's Pool Hall.

Boys wore jeans with pant legs rolled up, t-shirts with sleeves rolled up, and ball caps with Agri Chemical Company Logos and the caps bills were always to the front. Girls wore tank tops and cut-off jeans. You could tell if a girl's family had money, because she would wear a colored bra to match her tank top. Poor girls just had white bras.

The street in front of Aunt Nora's had many streaks of rubber imprinted in its pavement. There was always some one with a GTO or a Super Sport wanting to start a drag race. When the headers pounded out the sound of the 409 engine revving up, the pool hall would empty out and the race was on.

Drag races were matches fueled by testosterone and 200 Sunoco gasolines. Good ones were subject to legends, bad ones subject of police chases. My cousin Ezra owned a 1961 Chevy Impala Super Sport, 2 door hard top, white with red interior, 4 on the floor, dual quad, positraction. This car was never beat, as far as I know. To this day at family gatherings, the conversations always ventures over to "do you still have that Impala".

I learned a lot in that pool hall. I learned how to tell if the fix was on and a hustler was trying to take my hard earned money. Those experiences served me well in the Army. I never lost a months pay in a crap game the way some of my buddies had.

My colleague Dave remembers many misspent hours in his youth at the "Ball and Cue" in Coshocton. Dave said the pool hall had some amazing characters including "Dick the Rack". In those days the cost to play was tallied before the eight-ball rack was made, and Dick took the job seriously. Heaven forbid a player try to rack his own. That was tantamount to theft in office. We just didn't hear of that either. As Dave remembers, Dick was a gnome of a guy, but pretty happy, and really pretty good at racking. Dave remembers the sign on the wall that said "Own your own Cue; it will pay with better Play." Of course, few owned their own cues and in looking back, Dave doesn't think it would have helped his game. It sort of is like now. He could play golf with Tiger's clubs and still just be a hacker out for some public humiliation. Dave still had a great time misspending those hours, and wishes Dick well, wherever he racks today.

Just like my hometown, Coshocton is a river city; and as the song from Music Man say…"We got trouble right here in River City and it starts with P and is spelled POOL".

FUNERALS SHOULD BE FUN

—▯—

I had the honor of attending the funeral of a friend recently and it was a touching event. There was a eulogy at the church followed by the release of a dove near the burial site in the cemetery.

However, the first funeral I remember was sure a lot more fun. When my Uncle Cecil died, funerals were still held at the farm house. I remember going into the parlor with my grandmother to see Uncle Cecil's body. The room was full of daffodils and gladiolas of every color under the rainbow. The flowers were arranged in pots with handles and were stacked all the way to the ceiling. Some had ribbons with words, like Dear Brother or Rest in Peace. In the corner was Uncle Cecil's copper casket with light blue ruffled fabric. After grandmother said how good her brother looked, we moved into the next room, the dining room.

The mood in the parlor was sober; in the dining room the mood was festive. Two tables full of covered dishes and home made deserts filled the room. Neighbors, friends from Church and kin folk had been bringing food in all day. "Could you join us for a little Supper" the visitors were asked by one of the daughter-in-laws. "Oh, no we couldn't, we just ate", they all said. "Well, maybe just a small dish of Aunt Ada's Cherry Cobbler" one would say. "Good, we are cranking some home made ice cream on the back porch, be sure and get a scoop of Cousin

Ezra's egg custard ice cream to go with that cobbler."

It seemed half the county was coming by to pay their respects, and they certainly didn't let any food go to waste. Some of the men folk went to the back of the smoke house to wash down their food with some of Uncle Clyde's hard cider of some clear liquid in a jar. Uncle Clyde was holding court, getting friends and neighbors to reminisce about Uncle Cecil by telling stores about pranks they had shared. Seems Uncle Clyde was an intricate part of the grieving process, almost as much as the preacher (who was not allowed near the smoke house). Uncle Clyde would cut guys off if they got a snoot full.

For us youngins, the at home funerals were a great place to meet cousins, and play games. I had a crush on my cousin Carolyn Lynn. She was a third cousin and Uncle Clyde said that was far enough removed (allowing me to flirt with her). All the cousins assembled in the front yard and played dodge ball, red rover – red rover we dare you over, jump rope, and hide and seek. When the sun went down, we caught lightening bugs (fire flies). I put some of my lightening buys in a mason jar that was emptied by the men sipping with Uncle Clyde. I don't know what was in that Mason jar before, but it sure killed my fire flies.

After most of the callers had departed, the under taker got the family together to work out a schedule for staying up with the corpse. Carolyn Lynn and I volunteered for the first shift as others scurried off to do farm chores they hadn't been able to do during calling hours.

At first, it felt eerie in a room with a dead man. Carolyn Lynn eased her fears by talking and I just listened. When her brother came to relieve us, she gave me a big hug. A hug I have never forgotten.

It seems having funerals in your home was a lot of fun for cousins, but a strain on the rest of the family. That's why now days we use the services of a professional Funeral Director and their facilities. I read an article in the Schoedinger Dispatch a while back written about the Schoedinger family of funeral directors in Columbus. They did all the Irish wakes in the descendant's homes until the 1950's. They also operated hardware stores and sold furniture (they were good tie in business). Home funerals stopped because families got tired of friends and neighbors drinking up all their whiskey. Also some families had repairs to make or had to replace lamps, tables, etc. after the funeral because too much free drink caused a scuffle now and then. Those city slickers funeral directors could have used the services of Uncle Clyde. Uncle Clyde could keep funerals fun without things getting out of hand.

CITIZENS TO PAY MORE TAXES

These past few months, we have been bombarded with political ads promising to cut taxes for me, the middle class small business guy. That would be great because I pay Federal, State, and City Income Tax; Federal and State Corporate Tax; City Business Income Tax; Personal Property Tax; Business Personal Property Tax; Federal and State Unemployment Tax; Workers Compensation Tax; Social Security Tax Personally and as an employer; Sales Tax, Sales Usage Tax, and Gasoline Tax.

Apparently what I pay is not enough because the city is broke, the state says they can not balance their budget and fund the 22 state agencies, and the Federal government is printing more paper money, than carter has little liver pills. Here are some suggestions, at least for the City, so they can fill their empty coiffeurs and provide all those services we want them to.

Imported Bicycle Tariff – Tax everyone who rides a bike made in Taiwan, Japan, or China (I ride an American made bike). Go out to your garage and look at the Made in Decal on your bikes.

Nuisance Noise Tax – Tax all these teenagers that drive $500 cars with a $5,000 stereo system in the trunk, that when cranked up (none of these speakers and amps have a low setting) the woofers and tweeters vibrate the top layer of black top off the streets.

Stupid Talk Show Caller Tax – This tax would be liened against those idiots who call into the open public forum on WTNS. This could be a wind fall of monies to the city, not to mention the added benefit of cleaning up the air waves as some of theses callers have their life savings taxed away.

Political Littering Fines – The City would collect a fine from all the politicians who throw candy to the kids lining the side walks during parades on Main Street. The Surgeon General of the United States is trying to call attention to obesity in our children, while our leaders are giving away candy. Additionally, all the political yard signs still up, 48 hours after the polls have closed could have a tax levied against that particular politician.

Cigarette Butt Tax – Being an ex-smoker I can attest that this fine has the potential to bring in enough funds to repave every street in the city. Simply require a person who is buying a 20 pack of cigarettes, to turn in 20 cigarette butts, before they can buy a new pack. If they only have 10 butts to turn in that means they littered 10 butts and they would be fined $1.00 a butt or Ten Dollars.

Whiney Kid Tax – If you are caught in a public place (Church, Stores, and Restaurants) and your kid starts whining, you as a parent have 10 seconds to backhand your little brat so the rest of us can pray, shop, and eat in peace. One dollar per incident is not too much to ask. My father would never have been levied this fine. My father could drive our 1952 Chevrolet using his left hand, this freed up his right hand so he could slap me or one of my three brothers who all sat in the back seat. With four boys, he developed a backhand so good he should have taken up the game of Tennis. He had a better backhand than John McEnroe.

Express Lane Check Out Tax – If you are caught in the express checkout lane (where the sign clearly says 10 items or less) with more than 10 items, you will be taxed one dollar for every item over ten. We are all busy people, but some folks think they are too good to wait in the regular checkout line. They try to sneak a grocery cart full of items through the express lane.

I am sure there are many more worthwhile suggestions from other Tribune readers. I am sure the Mayor would love to hear from you too.

CYA–SOL

—▦—

Bernie Evers, the former CEO of WorldCom Tele-communications is being charged with nine felony counts of fraud. Bernie took the stand in court the other day and said he really didn't understand what was going on, that he didn't understand technical acronyms, like P.E. (price-earnings ratios). Bernie went on to say he was a P.E. Major (Physical Education) in College.

Not only was that statement unfair to P.E. teachers, but put a whole new meaning to what originally was a military term. C.Y.A. (Cover Your A--) was a military acronym coined to remind small unit commanders that they have to cover their rears from enemy flanking maneuvers. Bernie tried to C.Y.A. by saying he was just a dumb coach.

The military uses a lot of acronyms to embed messages in soldiers so they remember what to do without thinking. SASA (Stay Alert, Stay Alive) is an acronym to remind troops not to be daydreaming when on guard duty so a sniper doesn't sneak-up and take you out.

In paratrooper school, the Airborne Cadre constantly reminded us of what to do once the airplane door opened and we were to jump out. When the door opens, the wind and the aircraft engines make so much noise, normal voice orders can not be heard. Instead, hand signals, a green-red light, the Jumpmaster's boots, and acronyms were yelled out. A chaotic event comes off in a safe, orderly manner. "Stand up, hook up, shuffle to the door; jump out wide and count to four" was the chant we repeated when we ate breakfast, when we ran in formation, when we showered, when we slept (we chanted in our dreams). On the day of the first live jump, we didn't even have to think, we chanted and our bodies reacted involuntarily. There was no chance to back out, either, since the soldiers behind you were pushing forward and the Jumpmaster's boot was cocked and ready to assist you out the airplane door in case you balked. As you exited the aircraft, one last instruction was yelled, PLF. If you remembered to assume the position of Parachute Landing Fall (PLF) seconds before hitting the ground, chances were good you could walk away. If you failed in PLF you could be hauled away in the meat wagon (Army Ambulance) to the infirmary with a broken leg.

Everyday garrison life in the military requires one to master acronyms just to understand where to go and what to do. SSG Ricker once told me his 5/4 was DL so I was to take my POV to the PX and get some P38's to open our C's. Then I was instructed to see an E-5 at the MP for some C4 to warm our C's and an FM for a Prick 25. I was further instructed to not stop by the EM club for a couple of 3-2's because if I were late he would count me AWOL.

In civilian terms Staff Sergeant Ricker told to me his 1-1/4 (5/4) ton utility truck was dead lined (DL), so I was to drive my Privately Owned Vehicle (POV) to the Post Exchange Store (PX) and get some small can openers (P38's) so we could open our canned rations (C's). Then I was to see a Buck Sergeant (E-5) at the Military Police

(MP) building for some plastic explosives that get hot (C4) to warm our food. Also, I was to pick up a Field Manual (FM) for a handheld field radio (Prick 25). I was warned not to stop at the Enlisted Men's Club (EM) for a couple of 3-2's (Beer) because if I were late, I would be Absent With Out Leave (AWOL).

All military mess halls have sausage gravy on toast (SOS) for breakfast. Some Private First Class (PFC) who would rather have a donut for breakfast changed S.O.S. to Shi- on a Shingle.

Yesterday, I came home after a hard days work, hoping for a good home cooked meal. I was S.O.L., had a frozen TV dinner. S.O.S. would have tasted better.

How to Feed a Family

When times were tough, crop prices low and my father was laid off from his factory job, we tightened our belts. My little brothers got to wear "hand me down" clothes a little longer. Instead of new school clothes in September, my jeans were patched, socks darned and shoes resoled at the shoe repair shop. My father bought a set of hair clippers and a box of Bandaids, and we stopped going to the barber (the Bandaids were used for cuts while Father bettered his hair cutting skills). No store bought toys or trips to the movies, anything that required cash had to be given up. Food was a major expense for a large family and that is where we really saved money. Grits and Oatmeal became the only breakfast choices. We could feed our family of 7 for 50 cents in today's dollars. We got tired of it, but my mother would get creative by adding cheese to the grits, apples or raisins to the oatmeal.

Lunches of pinto or navy beans and cornbread were also cheap, but stuck to your ribs, made you feel full. Throwing in carrots and potatoes into the beans then mixing onions and mangos with the cornbread changed our attitude toward "beans again."

Supper was the meal we all ate together, precisely at 5 p.m... Our garden provided the entrees. Green beans, corn, tomatoes, cucumbers, new potatoes along with home made pickles and relishes were enjoyed with very little cost. The vegetables were the product of the good earth, our manual labor plus a little pride and perseverance. The only meat of the day was game I killed myself (rabbit, squirrel, quail or fish) and sometimes an old laying hen culled from the flock.

In the winter, the vegetables were fetched up from the root cellar, usually in quart glass Mason jars, jars we had canned and cold packed in the growing season on a stove in the summer kitchen. Winter meat was a part of a hog we had butchered in the fall and cured in the smoke house. I get hungry just thinking about what we ate. We made from scratch biscuits using lard we rendered from our hogs, bread made from 50 lb sacks of self rising flour. The Jam cakes used blackberries I picked myself. Peach preserves, dried apples, grape jelly, fresh eggs from our hen house, whole milk from our cows, and the list goes on. I bet our family of 7 lived off $10 dollars a week. We were poor, but proud. I knew I had responsibility. I knew I was useful, that my family depended on me to do my part and I depended on them to do their part.

Uncle Clyde told me that during the great depression, those that had extra food shared it with township trustees, who in turn gave to those families that couldn't quite make it on their own. Uncle Clyde said churches held all day preachin' and eatin' Sundays that helped feed the flock spiritually and physically. The haves and the have nots prayed and ate as equals and there was always plenty leftovers to take home.

Fast forward to now with food stamps and welfare checks. We have all been behind someone in the grocery checkout line getting T-bone steaks and shrimp and paying for them with food stamps. Uncle Clyde saw the transformation from churches and township trustees helping the poor, to the government handing down food stamps, subsidized housing, free medical care, free school lunches, a welfare check to cash and buy Nike shoes, CDs, car payments and movie tickets. Uncle Clyde quit school in the 8th grade because he had to work and help save the farm during the depression. It seems that an uneducated man figured out what is wrong with welfare and our educated politicians have not.

Uncle Clyde said "If you pay people to be poor, we will always have plenty of poor people". Once again, Uncle Clyde was right.

MILESTONES

—◨—

I have crossed many milestones in life. At age 16 when I got my drivers license, age 21 when I didn't have to drink 3-2 beer any longer, age 22 when I entered the Army, age 27 when I was discharged, and age 33 when I became a father. I am looking forward to the next big milestone, perhaps by age 70 something, grand father-hood.

Since grand fatherhood may well be my last milestone in life, I want it to be noted with some formality. I expect my future grandchild to refer to me as their "Grandfather". I don't want to be called "Gramps" or "Pop". It's ok for my grandchildren to refer to their parents as mom, dad, or whatever, but I want a more formal status.

I also want my grandchildren named after a family member, a president, or world leader; none of these modern names with funny spellings that parents either pull out of thin air or pick up from MTV, for my grandchildren. No Sharika, Ivory, Shyra, Teneka, Snoop Dog, Bono, or Carmen. Where do they come up with these names? When I introduce my grandchildren to a friend, I want to say something like, "This is my grandson Clyde; he is named after my Uncle who taught me how to fish and hunt; he was a good man. Or, I won't mind saying this is my granddaughter Eleanor, she is named after the former First Lady. Or even, this is Dwight, he is named

167

after the 5 Star General.

Being a baby boomer, coming of age during the free-thinking hippie era, I didn't think I would revert back to the ways of my un-enlightened parents.

But, here I am on the threshold of becoming a "Grand boomer". There is a web site that helps us grand boomers deal with the fact we are getting old and we need to share some of our world changing experiences with our grandchildren, mainly by writing narratives to go with family photos, sort of Kodak moments meets Lake Woebegone Days.

Here are some thoughts I plan on sharing with a Grandchild. (Picture of my family sitting in our parlor) "Those are my brothers and sister. Families were big back then because there was no good birth control. See the TV, it was black and white and only had 3 channels. We all wore white socks then. That thing my mother is wearing is an apron, women wore those back then because they cooked all the meals at home. That black thing on the end table is a telephone, it was the only phone in the house and we shared the same phone number with 16 other families.

Here's a picture of me in college having a party at my fraternity house, Alpha Gamma Pho. Yes, I had long hair and big bushy sideburns. Yes, I am afraid I smoked back then, although that's not a cigarette in this picture. You can tell girls were not into heavy makeup then, plus they didn't wear bras. No, that is not a dead person. That is Brother Leroy; he had too many "boilermakers". Yes, that's a peace symbol hanging on the leather string around my neck. That was the only kind of thong I knew of then.

This is my company picture when I was in Army Airborne School. Do I look scared? I wasn't scared. That's just my mean look. We all were supposed to look mean, not smile.

This car was called a Karman Ghia, that's me and your grandmother bringing your mother home from the Hospital. I didn't wear hats back then, I still had hair. Yes, I have a big smile on my face. It was the happiest day of my life. I think that's your grandmother's natural hair color, it's been so long I forget.

So, little Clyde, those are a few moments from your Grandfathers past. Next time we'll sit down with your mother's pictures and I'll tell you about some of her Kodak moments.

TELEVISION

—▣—

When I went away to college, my father pulled up to the dorm in our 1961 Pontiac, and I hopped out with my suitcase and alarm clock. I made it into my dorm room on one trip with room for my freshman welcome package.

My daughter moved into a newer and bigger apartment recently. It seems every time we take her back to college, it requires a larger vehicle. Her freshman year we filled a Minivan. By her senior year we used a full sized pickup and a Jeep. For grad school it was a U-Haul. If she does doctorate studies I may need a big rig.

Because of the move, she had to have newer furnishings. First on her list was a new big screen plasma TV. She wanted a newer bigger TV so she could have a "Friends" final episode party. She ruled out me helping her shop for a new TV when I told her I thought plasma was the blood product that winos sold to inter city blood banks. She doesn't think I am electronically savvy because I have been watching the same TV for the past thirty years. I have never watched an episode of Friends. My TV is never tuned to any network stations. My TV only receives the History Channel, CSPAN, CNN and ESPN.

We did not have a TV in our farm house until I was in High School. We did have a Philco radio with a beautiful walnut case; it was like a fine piece of furniture.

We picked up the local farm reports and obituaries in the morning. In the evenings when the reception was better, we picked up the Jamboree on WWVA out of Wheeling, the Opry on WSM out of Nashville, and Reds games on WLW out of Cincinnati.

When the farm no longer fed our growing family, my father took a job as a welder in the city. We rented a small house and bought a RCA Victor television. The RCA had a beautiful Philippine mahogany wood case. My father said all the walnut trees in this country were cut down, so the manufacturers started cutting down all the Philippine trees. We could even fix our RCA. If it went on the blink we pulled all the tubes out and took them to a "test your own" machine at the drug store, where we singled out the blown tube, bought a new tube, and fixed our TV.

Getting our TV to receive one of the three available stations was a feat in its own right. The rabbit ears antenna had to be elevated and turned in the correct direction to receive a particular station. It was a lot like bracketing in artillery shells in Army boot camp. Aim up, down, left, right, fire for effect. There wasn't a remote control device, but with only three stations to choose from, my father just used one of us kids to change the channel.

There was some great programming in the early days of TV. Instead of a perky sorority sister on the Today show, we had Dave Garaway and a chimpanzee. The Red Skelton Hour had an array of characters, but my favorite was a bum by the name of Clem Kiddelhopper. Art Linkletter's segment on his show, "Kids say the darndest things", was my father's favorite. Jack Benny and his side kick Rochester always tickled uncle Clyde's funny bone. When The Beatles were on Ed Sullivan, I cut Sunday Evening Bible Study. That was the only time I ever got into big trouble with my grandmother.

I do have some technological savvy. I can program a VCR. We use computers daily at the store. I am the owner of a Palm Pilot PDA. I like to sneak it into church and write with it before the sermon starts. I bet my grandmother would be turning in her grave if she knew I wrote stories in church. I bet she'd have watched Friends, too.

FAT KIDS

The Federal Center for Disease Control and Prevention recently sounded the alarms about obesity in our school children. Lack of physical activity and processed food for lunch were sited as leading causes for fat kids.

Growing up on the farm, I didn't have fat schoolmates. There were a few kids that were "big boned", but they were just big strong country boys who couldn't push away from the breakfast table. We all ate a big breakfast before school because we got up early to do our chores. On school days I still had to feed the chickens, slop the hogs and bring in firewood before breakfast. Parents wouldn't think of sending their kids off to school without a full belly. There wasn't a lot of variety to our breakfast, just good old fashioned food that "stuck to your ribs". Biscuits, Sausage, Ham and Eggs and fresh Milk were almost always the breakfast. For a change we had oatmeal or fried mush. Scrapple, cracklings, shoulder meat, and salt bacon were also on the table from time to time. We never had anything sweet for breakfast. In fact sweets (homemade pies, cobblers and cakes) were usually only served when we had company or the preacher came by after church. Everything came out of the hen house, the smoke house or the dairy barn. The meat and eggs were fried in lard using cast iron skillets. About the only thing we used for breakfast that was "store bought" was the Martha White self rising flour. The flour was purchased in 50 pound sacks. Once emptied the sacks were cut up and used for wash cloths, tea towels, or aprons.

With morning chores and breakfast done, I would pack my lunch bucket. My favorite was soup beans, ham, and corn bread leftovers. Ham and biscuits and a pear or apple out of our orchard were also very good. I always liked my apples peeled, so I sharpened my Barlow knife on Grandfather's honing stone. My grandmother canned her own home grown pimentos and mixed them with our own cow's cheese. With a pack of saltine crackers I had a meal and a snack for recess. No need to pack a beverage, our school had great water fountains, or we could buy a container of milk for 2 cents. I could never stomach factory milk having grown up on whole milk.

After school I rode my bike home. If it was raining, I was usually prepared. If the morning farm report forecast rain I would pack my rainsuit. Once in a while I got into a scuffle on the playground and got a paddling. The principal Mr. Williams had a wood paddle that looked like a small boat oar. If he gave me three "licks" with the paddle, he usually lifted me off the ground by the third swing. I pedaled my bike standing up going home on those occasions. What's worse, in a small county, my father usually knew by the time I got home of my paddling and he gave it to me again. My father didn't use a paddle, he just took off his leather belt and gave me a few "whacks".

So why are school kids fat now? They get up out of bed 5 minutes before the school bus stops in front of their house (no time for chores or home cooked breakfast).

They get to school and have a pop tart. For recess, some kids sit around and drink a Pepsi or Mountain Dew. Lunch entrees include Tater Tots, Sloppy Joes, Hot Dogs, Ice Cream and more Mountain Dew. After school the bus drops them off in front of their home, where they go in and eat Twinkies and play video games until a parent comes home and they order pizza. As Uncle Clyde would say, "As you sow, so shall you reap!"

POWER OUTAGE

I went home from work the other evening, only to find that a storm had blown a hugh tree across the electrical power line that fed our neighborhood. A lot of the neighbors were out in their yards, looking bewildered, hands in their pockets, looking up to the sky as if some divine guidance wold be forth coming on what to do with themselves while their homes were with out power.

I pulled into my driveway, and my wife too was standing in or yard looking up at the heavens. "No power and no cable", she says with that pitiful look on her face.

"I can't get the garage door up either", she whined. I suspect not being able to get in her car and drive somewhere to buy something we don't need was a major cause of her anguish.

"What are we going to do", she said to me and then glanced skyward.

I went inside the garage, pulled the electric garage door emergency release cord, and lifted the door manually. The wrinkles on her forehead vanished and she grabbed her car keys. She fired up the car, backed out of the drive and speed off for main street and second street to reconnoiter the storm damage and see which stores were open for business.

Meanwhile I walk into my house and the phone rings. It was a telemarketer wanting to talk me into switching my long distance phone carrier. Why is it that when mother nature unleashes a natural disaster such a storm or a tornado, the damn phones still work? I told the young lady calling that I do not have any authority to make any decisions regarding the running of my household, with the exception of the toilet and sewer lines. Any problems with a stopped up toilet or plugged sewer lines fall into my realm of responsibility; any thing else, my wife has to make the decision. With that said, I hung up and took the phone off the hook. If we were to be with out modern convinces, then we were to be with out the phone also. I saw prepared to get one with nature.

There I sat, in my porch swing enjoying the quite. There was a slight breeze in the air and that unique smell of freshness that comes along after a lightning storm. My mind drifted back to my youth, living on the farm with out a television. There are so many things you can do when not glued to the tv tube. Read the bible, or a book, crochet, whittle, or just watch and listen to the birds are some of the activities I enjoyed as a little boy sitting on the front porch.

As I was sitting I noticed a pair of squirrels (a male and a female) run up and down the powerless power line. They were engaged in a game of tag it appeared to me (really it was rodent fore play), when my wife returned from here execution to the part of town that had not lost power.

I could tell she was relieved. She had confirmed to herself that the end of the world was not at hand.

As she got out of the car she asked if I wanted to go

out to restaurant to eat tonight?

"Sure, lets go", I said. "I have to take a bath first", she said. I drifted back in time again to my youth and the fact that I only took a real bath on Saturday night, so I smelled good in Sunday school. I thought back to an Army maneuver I was on that precluded me from bathing for ten days. I thought to myself why does she have to bath twice a day? Then she called and asked if I could hold the flash light while she bathed.

Then it occurred to me that my wife and I should be doing what the squirrels were doing. I grabbed the flash light, uncorked a bottle of chable wine, a couple of glasses, two candles, put some cambert cheese on a plate and headed up the steps to the bathroom. I entered the bathroom, lite the candles and was prepared for an romantic encounter. My wife realizing what my intentions were, said, "What if the phone rings"? "No power", I said. "What if the door bell rings"? "No power", I said. "Play a Josh CD", she asked. "No power", I said "I'll sign". "You couldn't carry a tune in a bucket", she said and then started laughing.

Well things did progress and we enjoyed a wonderful evening together. I am looking forward to a summer filled with thunder storms; and power outages.

GIRLFRIEND VS. BIKE

I waited on a young man the other day in our Bicycle department. He really wanted to buy a new Cannondale Road Bike, but he also needed to buy his girlfriend a birthday gift; and he did not have enough money to do both.

A dilemma. I suggested he make a chart listing the attributes of one decision vs. the other (wife vs. bike). I learned this technique in a business class. This chart forces you to use an analytical approach, avoiding emotions, to reach the proper decision.

Before I get into the decision process this young man and I went through, let me assure the readers that I am a modern man. I am not a male chauvinist. In fact, I am ready to cast my vote for a woman President or Vice President. I was disappointed when George W. did not select Elizabeth Dole as his running mate in 2000 (perhaps he was afraid a Duke grad would show up his Yale sheepskin)? I will be disappointed again if George W. doesn't dump Dick Chaney for Condellsa Rice (perhaps that would void any options on Halliburton stock)?

Also, decisions in my house hold are made by mutual consent with my wife and daughter. Some may say that is being "hen pecked". To those I say, I learned in the Army that two against one is a tactical defeat, and one should retreat.

Girlfriend's Features   New Bike Features

Girlfriend's Features	New Bike Features
135 pounds (this is questionable)	18 pounds
Blonde, black roots	Jet Black/Raw Aluminum
"C" Cups	Two Water Bottles
Doc Martin Shoes	Continental Ultra Tires
Secretary Spread	Selle Royal Seat
Mood Swings	Shimano Derailleur
Compassionate	Cold Steel
Kate Spade Purse	Overland Panniers
Cranky	Dura ACE Crank
Loves Cats	Loves to chase Cats

Girlfriend's Maintenance   Bike Maintenance

Money, Make-Up, Hair Spray .... Air & Lube
Foundation, Lip Stick, Nail Polish,
Money, Conditioner, Oil of Olay,
Eye Shadow, Blush, Nair, Female
Hygiene Stuff, Money, Jewelry and .
Diamonds, Perfume, Nails and Manicures
Pedicures, Waxing, Tanning Bed Sessions,
Midol, Tampons, Money…

"OK, OK, I get the picture; I'll go to the bank and get the money, save me the bike."

CONGRESSIONAL JUNKETS

—▢—

The price of gasoline will cause many of us to change our travel plans this year. I know lots of folks who are going to stay home and work on their homes instead of driving to the beach for a vacation. I also know some folks for whom the cost of gasoline doesn't matter, because they don't have to pay what you and I do. These folks take vacations several times a year, to exotic destinations all over the world and they don't spend one red cent of their own money.

These folks are immune to the economics of day to day life because they don't have real jobs. They are congressmen. They disguise their taxpayer funded vacations by calling the trips junkets to gather information.

I first became aware of congressional junkets when I was a young soldier stationed in West Germany. In December the 1 st Infantry Division from Ft. Riley, Kansas would fly over in Air Force C5 cargo planes, pick up their pre-positioned war reserves, link up with my unit and others stationed in Germany and participate in a war scenior against a mock Russian Army. This was a well planned, technical maneuver involving thousands of soldiers and airmen.

This training exercise also involved hundreds of congressmen, who flew over on commercial jets with their wives and staff members to review the troops in action. After only an hour or so in the mud and breathing the diesel fumes from our tanks, the congressional entourage was off to Nurnberg or Munich for the Kris Kendal Mart (Christmas Shopping Market).

We soldiers went back to eating our C-Rations, sleeping in trucks and tanks, going un-bathed and using out door latrines. The congressmen stayed in the finest hotels, eating the best European cuisine, relaxing in the spa and using a bidet, all at taxpayer expense.

Unfortunately our Congressmen still use Junkets as a perk. The recent funeral of Pope John Paul II was attended by three U.S. Presidents and Dr. Condella Rice, our Secretary of State. That was the right thing for our country to do. The Pope, who championed freedom and democracy over the communist government of his native Poland, also warned against the excesses materialism of capitalism not bridled by morality. Pope John Paul's teachings about excesses must have fallen on deaf ears to the hundreds of congressmen, their spouses, and staff who travel to Rome for the funeral and other places of interest in Italy.

27 U.S. Congressmen make the taxpayer trip to Italy; I'm not sure how many Senators went too. I tried to contact my congressmen to see why he felt it was his duty to travel to Italy, at the tax payer's expense, he has not responded to my e-mail.

I called the Clerk of the House of Representatives which is the office that handles the congressional travel expenses. The clerk told me they have all the travel information for the Pope's funeral. I asked to see the itemized expenses and the itinerary of my representative, Bob

Ney. I was told if I came to their office in Washington I could review a summary of the trip. "I live in Ohio", I told her. "Could you fax or e-mail me a copy"? "No", she said I must personally come into the Washington D.C. office. I came right out and told her I thought I was getting the run around; the congressmen really want to hide how much they spend on their many travels. "That's the system" I was told.

Here is my recommendation to Congress that will help balance the budget and save social security. No more junkets! Stay home and work on your house; in fact, why don't all you congressmen replace the toilets in your bathrooms. Congressmen are so full of what toilets are used to flush down the sewer, I am sure they will enjoy the new water saver toilets that they required us to use by passing a stupid environmental law that was to have been a water conservation measure.

Country Boy Thesaurus

—◻—

My daughter was home from College last weekend. As she was unloading her laundry and raiding our pantry, refrigerator and freezer for food to take back to school, she left the door open to the garage. I called this to her attention as I have done many times by saying, "Were you born in a barn"?

Her response was, "Why can't you just say close the door? Why can't you just speak normal English?" She went on to say, "Could you write some of these witticisms down so I know what you are talking about? When my friends are over and you speak, it's like you are talking in a foreign language. Make me a country boy Thesaurus." I'll try to jot down a few I use now and then at work.

When speaking of someone who is slow to reach for their wallet when the check comes for a business lunch, I would say "he is tighter than a tick".

When I wait on a customer buying a fancy brass faucet for an old run down house, I think to myself, "He's trying to make a silk purse out of a sow's ear".

When a phone customer asks me how many different light fixtures we have I respond with, "As many as Carter has little liver pills."

To explain my social economic situation as a kid, I would explain it as "poor as a church mouse". When things get hectic in the store with the phone ringing and loading customer trucks, I feel like "a chicken running around with its head cut off". If I make a large sale, I stick my chest out and act "as proud as a Peacock". I bumped my head on a shelf the other day and the injured area got "red as a rooster's comb and as big as a goose egg".

When one of our part-time employees asked me why he had to clean the bathrooms again, my reply was because "cleanliness is next to Godliness".

My answer to an employee who hit his thumb with a hammer was, "can't you hit the broadside of the barn"? He didn't understand, but he's one that is "dumb as a fence post" anyway.

One of our young employees waited on his girlfriend's father and I could tell he was edgy. I told him he was "as nervous as a long tailed cat in a room full of rocking chairs".

When explaining to a female co-worker about our policy that women do the same physical work as men, my comment was "What's good for the goose is good for the gander." When she asked about more pay, I told her she was "still wet behind the ears" and needed more seniority. She asked me if she would eventually earn more pay, I said "Good Lord willing and the creek don't rise".

One of our employees hasn't been near a barbershop recently, so I asked him to "Get his ears lowered". He said he was satisfied with his appearance. I responded that he did look "Happy as a pig in slop". He remarked something about if he had a pay raise he could be better groomed and my come back was "Don't count your chickens before the eggs hatch.". When he muttered that he thought he could take me, I said that might be a "tough row to hoe". He said something under his breath to which I responded; "as we said in the Army, don't mess in your mess kit". I was also thinking "This boy hasn't got the sense God gave a Goose.".

So, I reviewed the above notes with my daughter and asked her, "Do you understand that my little sayings cause you to stop and think more about the situation?"

"Yes, thank you for sharing your thoughts." she said. I replied "No, No, Bless your little pea picking heart."

POTTY TRAINING

—⬚—

The other day our family went out to a restaurant for dinner. As we were looking over the entrées, a youngster at the next booth announced, "I have to potty!" The parents were embarrassed, but I laughed. I remember those years. Our daughter was a little slow in her transition from diapers to Big Girl underpants; but, once she got those training pants on, she knew what to do...train.

When she was growing up, we never went anywhere without Erika having to potty. Church, movie theater, grocery, bank, mall, didn't matter, she had to check out their restrooms; she had to potty train. If they offered potty training as an Olympic sport, my daughter's name would be on that green sign just outside of town. You've seen the sign that announces the celebrities who grew up here. Bob Brenley, World Series; Mike McCullough, PGA; Erika, Olympic Gold Medal Potty Training Winner.

Restaurants were her favorite training venue, and her favorite restaurant was Andy's. Since we were regulars there for Thursday night "all you can eat spaghetti", our favorite waitress (Sandy) learned to fit Erika's training regimen. We would be seated at our table and immediately Erika would announce she had to go to the restroom. Since Erika knew the layout of Andy's and we could see the ladies restroom door from our table, we let her "go" on her own. Sandy would come by our table and take my spaghetti order, my wife's fried chicken order, and then proceed into the restroom to take Erika's order. Sandy and Erika had developed a rapport. Sandy'd take a menu into the restroom, she and Erika would chat (talk big girl talk) for a few minutes and then Erika would order her usual, French Fries and gravy.

One evening at Andy's, I chided my daughter for her seeming fetish for checking out restrooms. Her come-back was "How did you potty train when you were a little boy, Daddy?"

I first had to educate her first about our two hole'r out-houses, and the fact that we had no indoor "restrooms" on the farm. I told her about being potty trained using a combinet for indoor "constitutions". I explained that the white porcelain coated pot, with cover, was hidden under the featherbed until called into action. I told her even adults pottied in the combinet; especially at night and if it was cold and rainy outside, you could reach for the "thunder mug, chamber pot or slopjar" and do your business without taking the path to the outhouse. That's how I started. First, I mastered the thunder mug and then I learned the path past the chicken coop to the out-house". She then wanted to know, how the potty came to be called "thunder mug?"

I knew that how the thunder mug got its nickname was not a topic I could cover as Sandy was bringing our dinner. I knew that, because my wife kicked me under the table. As I tried to side step the question, Erika dropped the bomb shell, "Where did you dump the poop after you pottied in the thunder mug, Daddy?" I learned in Lamaze class, or some where, that you should give honest answers to your child's questions.

"While standing on the back porch, my grandmother would pick up the pot, and with a lunge and a little wrist action, she would fling the contents out into the field by the chicken coop. Then the chickens would all run to see what had just landed in the grass and then proceeded to…" I caught myself as my wife threw down her fork in disgust. "What did the chickens do Daddy?"

"You will have to ask Uncle Clyde," I said, as my wife stormed past the waitress on here way out to the car. "Anything wrong with the fried chicken?" Sandy asked.

"Mommy wishes she had ordered spaghetti," Erika said.

TAX TIME

—◻—

April 15th is fast approaching and the air waves are filled with commercials trying to entice us with a tax service that will insure we receive a big fat refund. As the presidential campaign heats up, we are bombarded with politicians wanting to cut taxes for working families, small businesses, and farmers...haven't I heard this all before? Surely I fit into one of these groups the candidates want to help, but, I seem to be paying more and more in taxes, year end and year out.

I attended a County Commissioners meeting the other night. I didn't have an axe to grind. I just think it is something citizens should do from time to time. The County Auditor spoke at this meeting about property taxes. He started his presentation by saying he considered paying taxes to be a privilege of democracy. What a profound, if not difficult, statement to make to a group of citizens who had just received their property taxes and they did have an axe to grind. I nominate the man for a Bronze star with Oak Leaf Cluster because he sure got into a battle with those in attendance.

I, also consider it a privilege to pay taxes. I have lived in other states and another country and I like our system of government and taxes, warts and all, but I also still like to bitch about it too.

My Uncle Clyde had a good analogy about taxes which pretty well sums up my feelings. Uncle Clyde described each tax as a little piece of poop. Sales Tax, a little piece of poop; Property Tax a little more poop; Gas Tax more poop; Payroll Tax, Federal, State, and City, lots of poop; Workers Compensation Tax, Social Security Tax, Federal Excise Tax, poop, poop, and more poop. Uncle Clyde's analogy was "a little poop here, a little poop there, next thing you know, we have a crock of poop." (Uncle Clyde actually used the "S" word, but this is a family newspaper so I am substituting the "P" word for the "S" word).

Taxes are certainly complicated. That's the reason for the commercials for the preparers. I had a recent experience to drive that point home. I had the privilege of undergoing a state sales tax audit. I equate this audit to other unpleasant experiences in life. It was as bad as having to take a bath on Saturday night as a kid. It was as bad as having a pimple outbreak before a date in High School. It was as bad as cleaning out the mess hall grease trap during K.P. in Army boot camp. It was as bad as changing my kids diaper the first time. None of this was life threatening, but certainly was not a golden moment either.

Here are some examples of findings from my audit. A farmer was not allowed to avoid sales tax on bags of concrete to repair a fence post. If he had bought the concrete to set a new fence post, it would have been tax exempt.

A trucking company was allowed to avoid sales tax on bolts they purchased to repair a truck. Truckers pay a PUCO tax plus fuel tax, therefore no sales tax on bolts.

However, the trucking company must pay sales tax for windshield wiper fluid or paper towels.

A family from a Licking County Farm bought three expensive ($750.00 each) mountain recumbent bicycles for use in "chasing down cattle" without paying sales tax, but had to pay sales tax for the batteries they purchased to go in the bicycle speedometer.

A small factory purchased some fans this summer to cool the work area, this was tax exempt. They purchased fly swatters to kill flies swarming around the employees too, but the factory had to pay sales tax on the fly swatters.

So, you see....Uncle Clyde was right. Taxes are a crock of poop.

FARM DIET PLAN

—◻—

Obesity is a major health concern in the U.S. today. Dieting is by far a major growth industry in our country. The Adkins Plan is probably at the top of the heap. The marketing geniuses at Adkins are now flooding the media with ready made meals, snacks, and drinks that are billed as being delicious, but will not cause you to gain weight. I look for George Jetson to come out with a line of diet foods next. The Jetson's ate little pills to take care of their daily nourishment. The U.S.D.A. has a proposal to require more detailed labeling on the foods we buy, including fast foods. The government wants to study our foods more.

For crying out loud, enough is enough. Food is the sap of my soul. Food is like sex, if you study it clinically it loses its savor.

I long for the food of my youth. "If it ain't greasy or sweet, it ain't fit to eat", was the way my grandfather felt about food. I miss tender turnip greens out of the garden cooked slowly with a ham hock. I loved fresh stewed tomatoes made with plenty of crumbled white bread crumbs and lots of sugar. Oh how I miss red eye gravy made from county ham drippings, poured over "made from scratch" biscuits with lard! Corn on the cob soaked with real butter, cabbage slaw with sugar-vinegar dressing, black eyed peas cooked with a little jowl bacon and onions, and cherry cobbler with big hunks of dumplings, sprinkled with sugar and a big glob of real butter on top to soak its way to the bottom. Wash all this down with "Baptist Beer" (Iced Tea)!

Why weren't we obese back then? I'm not sure how many grams of fat and carbs were in the meal I just described. We did not have calculators then, so to add those kind of calories would have required a sharp #2 pencil and much "carrying" as we called the arithmetic process.

No one in our family was fat, except Uncle Clyde did have a big belly. Grandmother said that was because he spent more time chasing women instead of doing farm chores. We did not have expensive home gym equipment. Instead of a treadmill, we had to walk to the Pascal General Store every day to sell eggs (2 miles round trip). No free weights either, digging postholes with a spud bar and earth auger worked our upper torso. We were without a stationary bike, I had a real bicycle to chase down cows that got out of the pasture and were headed down the lane for Mr. Richardson's alfalfa field. Bow flex was not on infomercials yet; we used a bow saw, cross cut saw and a double bit axe to cut fire wood for the winter. For more bicep definition, we used a sledge and a wedge to split kindling wood. No aerobics classes either; we had a snath and a scythe to clean out fence rows. We used no stress balls; we shelled beans by hand instead. No stair stepper to works our legs, several trips a day from the cellar to the kitchen, from the kitchen to the garden, from the kitchen to the attic were enough to get our heart rate up.

We didn't "sleep in" either. You don't sleep in when

you have a small herd of cows to milk twice a day. Couch potatoes we were not. We didn't even have a couch, only rocking chairs and a settee in the parlor. We weren't glued to the "tube" every day either. We didn't have a TV, only a radio to learn of current trading prices of beans, corn and tobacco, and of course to hear if a neighbor had died. The phrase "no pain, no gain" is used today to describe the process of losing weight and staying in shape. Our phrase could have been "eat hardy, work hard".

TEN COMMANDMENTS

There has been a lot of debate in recent media forms about the removal of the Ten Commandments Monument at an Alabama Court House. The debate comes about because of gray areas. Religion isn't simple to understand. If is not always black or white, but shades of gray.

I was fortunate, however, to have my Uncle Clyde explain the Ten Commandments in such away that at 10 years of age, they made a lot of sense. He taught me how to remember the "Thou-Shalt-Nots" by giving examples of things I knew something about.

Thou shalt have no other gods. Uncle Clyde explained that when he was in the Army in the South Pacific there were folks who worshiped big stone statues of bald fat men. He said they looked like Uncle Cecil in his underwear.

Thou shalt not make idols or bow down to them. Uncle Clyde said some folks were too wrapped up with Elvis (Pelvis Elvis) and they fell into breaking this commandment. However, he worshiped Jane Mansfield and kept a picture of her in the smoke house.

Thou shalt not use the name of the Lord in vain. I never heard the Lord's name used in vain much until boot camp in the Army. Uncle Clyde taught me how to use words that were "cool" but wouldn't send you straight to hell. Gosh darn, Dag Nabbit, Dog Gone, Golly, Holy

Mackerel are just a few that accentuated the moment, but was not disrespectable to the Lord.

Remember the Sabbath day, keep it holy. Not only does that mean going to Sunday school, it means taking a bath on Saturday night. This commandment could be twisted and be used to get out of chores on Sunday.

Honor they father and thy mother. Don't back talk to your parents. They brought you into this world and they can take away your bike, sling shot and make you take a bath every day, if they so desire.

Thou shalt not kill. This one took some explaining. Of course I knew you were not to kill another human being, but what animals you could kill was up to interpretation. It's OK to kill crows, but not redbirds? Killing ground hogs is good but not a chipmunk? Don't step on a Toad, but gig Bull Frogs (they are good eating). Then Uncle Clyde talked about it being OK to kill when you are in the Army. See what I mean, another gray area.

Thou shalt not commit adultery. I knew about the birds and the bees (barnyard version), but this adultery thing was hard to understand. Uncle Clyde said if your wife caught you committing adultery, your wife could kill you, but wouldn't that break commandment #6?

Thou shalt not steal. That was easy to understand in terms of money and things, but Uncle Clyde said there were exceptions. You could steal someone's favorite fishing hole or watermelons from mean widow Miss Ollie's garden. You could steal a kiss, if she let you. But, how is it stealing if she let you?

Thou shalt not bear false witness against thy neighbor. No lying to the Game Warden when he asked if Billy Joe Richardson has been poaching deer with a flashlight at night. Like wise when questioned by Mrs. Martin about who threw turnips at her nephew, do not falsely accuse Billy Joe Richardson when in fact it was you and Bobby Ray.

Thou shalt not lust for your neighbor's house or his wife. Lusting after Mrs. Richardson was never going to happen, as Uncle Clyde said "that woman must have been hit by an ugly stick". Lusting after Billy Joe's motorcycle was a sin I am guilt of, even today.

Uncle Clyde's examples were intended to make the commandments black and white, but they left me very much in shades of gray.

HUNTING SEASON

—◻—

Hunting season has started and our county is being invaded by city slickers from Cuyahoga, Stark, and Franklin Counties. Some invaders arrive in humongous motor homes, traveling like country music stars. They all have thousand dollar shotguns, camouflage clothing and snoot of booze. I could never understand why they try to be one with nature, yet they continue to wave a big lodge ring, wear gold chains around their neck and smell like a tavern. I am sure the deer get a good laugh at some of these city slicker hunters. Many are illiterate also; they can't read "No Hunting" signs posted on fence posts around farmers' property.

I remember when I first bagged some game by myself. The day came one July when I was twelve. Grandfather and I had walked to the store and sold some eggs. He gave me the money to buy a brick of 22 long rifle hollow point bullets and said he had a hanker'in for squirrel. When we returned to the farm, I ran into the house, grabbed that old single shot bolt action Salvage rifle, and headed for the patch of hickory trees behind the barn. I had my eye out for an old fat red squirrel I had seen there many times. Squirrel season was a couple months away, but grandfather said a man can do what he wants on his own land.

I arrived in the woods and began barking like a female squirrel, as grandfather taught me to do. Soon, sure enough, that old fat red squirrel came swinging from tree to tree to see what was going on. I felt sweat running down my forehead and my heart was racing 100 miles an hour. It was like I was on a big game hunt and had a tiger coming at me. I caught my breath and just watched that old fat red squirrel. After a while he figured out there were no females barking for him, so he proceeded to scratch around the floor of the woods looking for hickory nuts. He found a big one that was half cracked open, and began to eat his tasty find. I lowered the open sights on my rifle. Although it was the middle of the summer, I swear I could see my breath as I took aim on old fat red. I squeezed the trigger as grandfather had shown me until "crack" the rifle discharged, a little smoke came out of the barrel and my heart was pounding out of my chest.

I stood up; my legs trembling, and ran over to where Red had been eating that nut. Sure enough, a few feet away lay Red, stretched out on a bed of Pawpaw leaves. I poked him with the barrel of the rifle, just to make sure he wasn't playing possum. I picked up old Red by the tail and ran back to the farm house. Grandfather helped me skin'm and cut up the meat. I nailed the bushy red tail to the door of the smoke house, for all to see.

When we where finished; grandfather made me wash my hands in rubbing alcohol, "to kill the squirrel fever germs". I had seen my father also rinse his hands after dressing game, but he always used Heaven Hill Bourbon. When I took the squirrel meat into grandmother I asked her about this squirrel fever. She explained it was a disease transmitted by the blood in animals and could make you deathly ill.

Grandmother reiterated that one should clean their hands with rubbing alcohol after skinning any game. I told her my father always used bourbon to clean his hands. Grandmother turned red in the face and said "I suppose he said the bible said to use bourbon". Yes, I said, how did you know? Grandmother said "your father always quotes the bible when he has done something wrong". "He picked that up from your Uncle Clyde.

Hurry Up and Wait

———

I was talking to an old schoolmate by phone the other evening. We both promised to get together soon. The reality is we are too busy. If we are all so busy, why do we spend half the day waiting?

I had a doctor's appointment the other day that ate up over an hour of just waiting in the waiting room. I remember going to the doctor when I was a kid. Doc Martin had a farm with an attached office, about 10 miles from our farm. He had office hours, but if you needed him after hours, you just called and told him you were coming. I once had a grasshopper fly up and hit me in the eye. My eye was swollen shut and I could not see. After the cold wash cloth soaked in Epsom salts failed to take down the swelling, it was off to Doc Martin's. It was Saturday night and he was playing cards and smoking a pipe with some friends in his dining room. When my father knocked on the door, Doc's wife led us to the office. Doc threw his cards into the pot and came right in to see me, no waiting. A little small talk about this year's corn crop and the price of cattle preceded his examination of my eye. Doc assured my father that with the application of a salve he gave me and more cold compresses, I would be fine in the morning. In fact, he said, I could still make it to Bible School. You had to have a very high fever or be dead to get out of going to Bible School on Sunday. My father offered to pay when we got our milking check, but Doc said a couple of my Grandmother's Custard Pies would do just fine.

The other day I had to pick up my wife at the Columbus Airport. I showed up at the airport an hour early and the flight was an hour late. I remember my first airplane ride at age 8. I flew Trans World Airlines to Wilmington, N.C. to my namesake uncle. My father drove me to the airport, ten minutes before the departure. I had one small suitcase and we walked out onto the tarmac and up a flight of rolling metal stairs. My father gave my ticket to a young, pretty stewardess who promised she would take care of me since I was flying alone and it was my first flight. The plane was noisy and you could see into the cockpit with all the instruments and dials. All the men passengers wore suits and the ladies wore hats. There were no TV's or audio equipment on the plane for the passengers, everyone brought a book to read. Before the pilots revved up the engines, the stewardess gave us the flight safety instructions. Every passenger stopped what they were doing and focused on the emergency procedures. Everyone's head turned as we followed the directions to the two emergency doors. I paid particular attention to the rear bathroom. We still had an outhouse at home and I was bound and determined to "hold it" until I got to Wilmington. I was not going to use a flush toilet 10,000 feet in the sky. After we took off the pretty stewardess brought me a coke and a bag of peanuts. She smelled so good, I was in love. After the coke, I couldn't hold it any longer, I held up my hand and the stewardess came to my seat. I explained that I was not familiar with indoor plumbing much, and especially on an airplane. She took my hand and led me to the rear of the plane. She told me to just go in, close the door and do what I would do at home. I asked if there was anyway I could fall through the seat, out of the airplane and hit the ground below. She assured me I would not fall out, but just to make sure, I could leave the door open a little and she would wait outside for me. I did and overcame my fear of flying. When we landed, my Uncle Tom was parked on the tarmac. No waiting.

WELCOME OHIO'S FIRST LADY

—▫—

Much has been said about Ohio's new Governor growing up on a small dirt road in southern Ohio in a place called Duck Run. The Governor's wife, Ohio's First Lady, grew up near my childhood home in Kentucky. Frances Strickland grew up on a dirt road, too. Her home town newspaper headlines recently read, "Ohio First Lady is both Buckeye and Bluegrass, Can that be legal?" She knows as many Kentucky-Ohio and Ohio-Kentucky jokes as anyone else (yes, people in Kentucky make fun of Buckeyes because they talk funny). Frances lived and worked on her family's dairy farm. Frances knows what it is to get up at 4:00 a.m. to milk the cows and then do it all again at 5:00 p.m., seven days a week, with no sick days, or vacations, living from milk check to milk check.

Frances spent many an hour fetching posthole diggers, milk filters, feed supplements, bag balm, or Carhartt overalls from Metzger's County Store. When the rare city slicker ventured off the paved roads and got stuck in a mud hole on the lane in front of their farm house, Frances would hook up the Farmall Tractor and pull them back onto dry road bed.

Yes, Frances knows a thing or two about hard work, chores, and the all-day "preachin' and eatin'" Sundays at the Simpsonville Methodist Church. Her father made her practice her softball pitch and her mother made her practice the piano, so along with farm chores, there was

205

no time to get in trouble.

Frances resisted the trend to get married and stay barefoot and pregnant. Instead, she went to college and ended up marrying a fellow Ph.D candidate who got into Ohio politics and is now Governor. Ironically, one of Frances' hometown girl friends also left the farm, and Martha Layne Collins became Kentucky's first woman governor.

Dagmar Celeste, wife of Dick Celeste, the last Democrat to serve as Ohio Governor, asked Frances whether she plans to produce a First Lady cookbook. Frances answered that her early years were spent farming and not in the kitchen. Frances did say she could write a pamphlet on "50 Different Ways to Fix Grits." If you don't know, grits is a farm breakfast staple that sticks to your ribs and gets you through till dinner time.

This past year we have witnessed many "dumb" deeds by our Ohio politicians. I am hoping some fresh-faced, down-home folks, both born on dirt roads, will produce a renewed respect for elected officials. In America there are often two roads to travel. You can be born with a silver spoon in your mouth, go to Ivy League colleges and use your family name to be elected Governor or President (the paved road) ; or you can come from hard scrabble, pull yourself up by your boots straps, work hard and also become Governor or President (the dirt road).

Since Frances is a farm girl, I hope she gives this advice to her husband. If the Governor is asked to skip work for a day and be wined and dined at an exclusive

Columbus Golf Country Club by lobbyists interested in receiving state construction contracts under the table, I hope she steps in. I hope Frances will use her country girl upbringing and tell the Governor, that golf is an idle game played on grass that should be allowed to grow and make hay to feed dairy cows. The only reason to leave work is for funerals or a sale down at Metzger's Country Store. Furthermore, a Governor should not run with men who don't have calluses on their hands and who grew up on paved roads.

If she needs to fire up the old Farmall to drag the Governor out of the mud, she can do it. Ohio has spent enough time in the mud.

LET'S GO FISHING

A friend asked me to go up north to Canada with a group of guys to fish. I had to respectfully decline because I have not had much success in the past on these male bonding fishing expeditions.

I did fish a lot as a kid. That was one of my chores on the farm, to catch a mess of fish once in a while to put on the supper table. I always fished with red worms I dug with a grub hoe in a shady spot behind our out house. My fishing pole was a Sassafras tree sapling I cut while clearing fence rows with a brush axe and scythe. I bought the fishing line and fish hooks at the Western Auto in town using my portion of Grandmother's egg money. I made my own sinkers using a mold and the lead weights from car wheels. The bobber was just a chunk of corn cob. I fished from the banks of various farm ponds. On hot summer days, I skinny dipped with the fish to cool off. I once caught 22 smallmouth bass in Mr. Richardson's pond and we had a fish fry for all the hands that helped us put up hay that weekend.

My first bad experience fishing was while I was stationed at Ft. Carson, Colorado. A group of us rented fly fishing equipment and went to a state park that was also a Buffalo sanctuary. Trying to fly fish without lessons turned out to be a joke. The fly spent more time landing on my head or hooked into one of the guys getting into the cooler of Coors beer behind me than it did landing on the water in front of a hungry lake trout. Signs all over the parked warned of the dangers of messing with the buffalo and said the park closed at sundown.

Maybe we were having too much fun hooking ourselves, or maybe it was the Rocky Mountain Water in the Coors, but we lost track of time. As we stumbled through the dark carrying our gear and three small trout back to our cars, we discovered we had parked in a Buffalo herd's favorite night time spot. The herd had nested down for the night. Rather than cause a stampede, we started walking the 15 miles back to the park entrance to call for help. Luckily a park ranger came along and professionally shooed away the Buffalo so we could drive back to our base, but not without first giving us a citation for keeping three undersized trout.

My next bad fishing experience was while on a duty assignment at Ft. Bragg, N.C. The Army's recreational services were sponsoring a deep sea fishing trip and it was rumored that a bunch of Army Nurses had signed up. I went only to find out there were only two nurses on the boat. The skipper only allowed 3.2 beer, which made us drink twice as much. After we were out about 5 miles, a storm came up and tossed that fishing boat around like an apple bobbling in a galvanized wash tub. I started sweating, and then got the chills, the shakes, my skin turned white and then I lost my breakfast and all the beer. I could not stand up. I just curled into a fetal position on the deck. After the rain quit, the skipper came over to me and asks me if I felt any thing hairy in my throat. "No, Why?" I said. He said that I had puked up every thing except my butt hole, so if I felt something hairy, swallow; he didn't want me losing my butt on his boat. Boy, did he think that was funny.

With those experiences, if someone asks me to go fishing, I tell them all the fish I want comes from Bakers Foods or Buehlers.

I WILL HAVE THE
RED HOT DOG, PLEASE

—⊡—

I participated in a strategic Army War Game once in Germany; when I did what most G.I.'s do, go where we are told not to go. Three of us sneaked away from our tent and went into the nearby little village that was "off limits". If the Army declared an area "off limits" it was like waving a red flag in front of a bull, we just had to go there. There was a brothel in this little town of Steinenbronn which is why it was off limits. After two weeks of eating C rations, we were more interested in getting a good hot meal at a restaurant. Besides, we didn't have enough money for the house of ill repute anyway. We found a little Gastehaus on the edge of town. It was a family business. The family lived up stairs and operated a little restaurant down stairs. The father cooked, the mother was the waitress and their two young boys just peaked around the corner looking at the funny American soldiers.

Most restaurants in Europe have menus printed in at least four languages (German, French, Spanish, and English). Most, but not this restaurant. Their menu was hand written in German. My buddies and I could only order one item in German, beer. The lady asked us for our food order in German and I spoke for my buddies by saying "Ich bin dumm kopf" (we are dumb Americans), then I said in English, "Just bring us something good to eat". The lady must have understood what I said because after several beers, she brought three different entrees.

My grandmother was of German heritage and I recognized all three meat entrees. My two Army buddies were city boys, and I knew they wouldn't eat the meal if they really knew what they were, but my buddies had more beers than I had. I was staying sober, because I had to read the compass in order to get back to our bivouac.

I had the lady give Leroy the "steak". "Doesn't look like any steak I ever had", Leroy said. "It's fixed German style", I told Leroy. He ate it and enjoyed it. It was actually Raw Steak Tartar (raw ground beef with onions, spices, capers, and raw egg on top).

"Give Bernie the "red hot dog", I told her. It was a Blood Wurst (spices, blood, and meat stuffed into an intestine casing). Bernie thought it was a bit spicy, but washed it down with more beer.

Bernie and Leroy would not even look at my meal. "Looks like shoe leather", Bernie said. It was actually beef tongue, tender and delicious. After we finished our meal and paid. The German family, including the little boys came out and thanked us, in English. They spoke very good English. They had just let us stumble along making hand signals and speaking English with a German word thrown in here and there. I asked the lady if they had many American guests. "Yes, she said, last night we had a squad of M.P.'s (military police) stop in and eat".

Then it dawned on me; here we are, in an off limits village and the M.P.'s could stop by any minute. We said our good byes, and gave the little boys Chicklet chewing gum we had saved from our c rations. Outside we got our bearings and I shot an azimuth back to where we had exited the woods. We stumbled through the dark back to our Platoon's bivouac. The First Sergeant hadn't missed us, so we were not in trouble.

The next day I told Leroy and Bernie exactly what we had eaten. "Man, how could you let us eat that stuff" Bernie said. Leroy said "you dumb country boys will eat anything". I told them "you smart city boys let me order".

MY LITTLE RED
RADIO FLYER WAGON

About my fifth birthday, I received a metal Radio Flyer wagon as a gift from my Uncle Clyde. My birthday party consisted of a Jam Cake my grandmother baked and carton of Neapolitan Ice Cream. I loved Sealtest Neapolitan Ice Cream because it consisted of three flavors; vanilla, chocolate, and strawberry. My grandmother sliced it so each piece contained all three flavors. My party was held on the front porch after church. I received wonderful presents. My grandfather gave me a Barlow knife. My father gave me a bag of marbles and Uncle Clyde gave me a Radio Flyer Wagon.

The wagon was not new. It had belonged to an older cousin. Uncle Clyde said Radio Flyers were built like a brick outhouse (although he used a different word), which meant they were heavy duty. Uncle Clyde had sanded the bed, repainted with fire engine red Fix All Enamel Paint and put on a new set of wheels. It looked brand new to me.

For my next birthday my family pitched in and bought me a brand new Huffy Sting Ray Bicycle. It had a banana seat. My Huffy was purchased at the Western Auto on Main Street. Huffy bikes were made in Dayton, Ohio by a fellow who was friends with two brothers who had been in the bike sales and service. In fact the brothers sold some Huffy bikes before they branched off into the airplane business (Orville and Wilbur Wright). My Huffy bike could go anywhere on the farm, as long as I could pedal, but it did require some maintenance. Grandfather taught me how put grease on the chain and axles, how to patch tubes punctured by a thorn and how to adjust spokes to fix bent rims.

I loved going to Western Auto with my father. I would look over the bike and fishing supplies while my father tried out power tools. Unless the price of raw milk was up, giving us a little extra money, my father usually bought a ball of string and just dreamed of buying a shop full of power tools.

Today people don't wait for a bigger milk check to buy things. Today people just "put it on plastic". Today we don't want to spend a week's pay for a bicycle or sell a beef or a pig to buy a table saw or hammer drill. We all started buying from big stores, like K-Mart. They were cheaper than Western Auto. That was great, but we wanted things cheaper yet. Sam Walton came along with the Wal-Mart Stores that sold merchandise at "low price every day".

Western Auto and many other small businesses are gone now. K-Mart is in and out of Bankruptcy Court. However, there are plenty of cheap products on retail shelves. Isn't that wonderful?

Well, now we have another problem. All the folks who eventually left the farm for good paying factory jobs in the cities are getting laid off because of outsourcing. Huffy Bicycles were all made in Ohio factories until Wal-Mart came along and told them to make a cheaper bike than K-Mart had. Huffy complied by importing and outsourcing. Huffy tried to maintain their frame factory and assembly in Ohio; but, in the end that wasn't enough to satisfy demands for cheaper and cheaper products. Huffy gave up and began outsourcing everything to China. Celina, Ohio was no match for Shanghai.

Today 3-31-04, another great American Manufacturer announced they are shutting down their Chicago factories and outsourcing everything to China. Radio Flyer said they could not use American labor, benefits, work and environmental rules and meet the price points people were willing to pay for their little red wagons.

An Uncle Clyde would say, "It doesn't matter how cheap it is if you don't have a job and don't have any money".

Made in the USA
Charleston, SC
25 October 2010